# Burslem

## in Words and Pictures

Joseph Boulton, born October 21 1872, died about age 60.
He is pictured to the rear of 12 Stanfield Road (off Hamil
Road), Burslem. *Courtesy of Jean Wood.*

## Mervyn Edwards

# To My Parents

## Acknowledgements

I am indebted to numerous people connected with the Burslem area who have assisted in the production of this book, and most are credited in the book. I would like to thank the following people for their assistance or interest:

Kenneth Edwards and Bernard Frain for proof-reading; Mark Heath and the girls at Thirty Minit Photo at ASDA, Wolstanton; Pat and Derek Barnard, Stitch In Time, Market Place, Burslem, for keeping a register of interviewees for me; Harold Harper and Nigel Coulton for approaching potential interviewees. Also: Glenys Adams, B. Baker, Sheila Carter, Mrs Cotton, Mrs Dakin, Mrs J.M. Morris, Mr Potter, David Riley, Miss Robertson, Mrs O. Skelding, Derek Taylor and Father Bryan Williams.

Where photographs have been borrowed, every effort has been made to credit the original source. Some have been purchased from craft fairs and secondhand bookshops in either original or copied form. If we have failed to acknowledge anyone in the production of this book, an apology is offered. The trade advertisements reproduced in this book are from The Burslem Traders' Association Souvenir Programme to commemorate the Coronation of Queen Elizabeth II (1953).

**Also by Mervyn Edwards:**

**Potters at Play**
**Potters in Pubs**
**Potters in Pits**
**Potters in Parks**
**Great Pubs around Stoke-on-Trent**
**Wolstanton in Words and Pictures**

**All published by Churnet Valley Books.**

**CHURNET VALLEY BOOKS**
1 King Street, Leek, Staffordshire. ST13 5NW 01538 399033
thebookshopleek.co.uk
© Mervyn Edwards and Churnet Valley Books 2004
ISBN 1 904546 14 5

Printed and bound by Bath Press

# CONTENTS

Mervyn Edwards was born in Newcastle-under-Lyme in 1961 and became a Green Badge Tourist Guide in 1989. He worked at the now-defunct Chatterley Whitfield Mining Museum for four years, becoming Assistant Education Officer, and is well-known in North Staffordshire as a tutor for the Workers' Educational Association.

He has had numerous articles on local history published, as well as six previous books. Mervyn is a familiar voice on Radio Stoke, Spokesman for the Potteries Pub Preservation Group and a regular columnist in CAMRA's Potters Bar newsletter. He is also a pen and ink artist and cartoonist and has completed 16 Potteries Marathons.

Smallthorne Baths in 1938. Emily Boulton and Florence Nevitt.
*Courtesy of Jean Wood.*

# INTRODUCTION

*"The past is a foreign country: they do things differently there."*

L. P. Hartley.

The success of my previous book, Wolstanton in Words and Pictures, has prompted this second volume of reminiscences. It covers Burslem and its environs: Longport, Dale Hall, Middleport and Cobridge. This is an area which teems with history. What's more, there is a great passion for local history in the neighbourhood, and this finds its focus in the once-monthly meetings of Burslem History Club. Many of its members have helped in one way or another with the production of this book.

Each of the contributors agreed to be tape recorded in good faith, and transcripts have been checked and revised in order to minimise the possibilities of slips-of-the-tongue, or misunderstandings on the part of the author. Accepting the fact that the memory can play tricks, and that collecting oral evidence is a practice which occasionally presents pitfalls, an effort has been made to corroborate and cross reference as far as possible - hence the footnotes at the end of some of the chapters.

In many respects, the way we view and explain the past is just as important as our ability to recall dates and details. For example, Eric Sherratt traces the demise of Waterloo Road as a self-contained community almost separate from the town of Burslem, from the time when the new housing estate was built at Norton.

Some of my interviewees have exercised the privilege of late middle age by comparing the supposed innocence of the mid 20th century with today's perhaps more competitive society. In producing the following transcripts, I have spared the reader much of this type of nostalgia, and allowed the interviewees' descriptions of 'the way we were' to highlight the differences between fifty years ago and the present day. Dewy eyes behind rose-tinted spectacles combine to impair our vision as well as fog our powers of recall. Incidentally, Geoff Weaver was brutally frank about aspects of his childhood: *"Never mind today's vandalism. We were buggers as children"*.

It has also been my objective with the transcripts to allow the particular personality of the interviewee to shine through. The words used by, for example, Robert Adams, reflect his own personality and sense of humour, which I think is important in conveying his perspective of bygone Burslem. Where my interviewees have spoken on the same topic (there are several memories of the local schools in this volume) I have been happy to let them do so. 'Duplication' of material has created the opportunity for me to corroborate and compare my findings, and I believe the reader will find this an interesting process.

The aim has been to create a community project which will engender discussion and further contributions. The author can be contacted through Churnet Valley Books, and would welcome any further reminiscences about the area from those who know it well. Any photographs offered can be copied quickly and returned to their rightful owner.

ST. JOHN'S CHURCH, BURSLEM

MERVYN EDWARDS 2001

Princes Square, Longport, probably in 1950s.

Hamil Road Clowes Methodist Church on the corner of Hamil Road and Gordon Street.
The foundations are being laid.

Holy Trinity Church, Hamil Road.
The departure of Henry Ellis Briscoe in
August 1977.  He had been the priest
there for 15 years.
*Courtesy of Jean Wood.*

Princes Square, Longport, c. 1940.
John William Davies.

The Old Town Hall in the
Market Place

The official opening of
Ceramica. (17/6/03)

The Cenotaph, Swan Bank,
with the Red Lion to the rear, 1957.
From L-R:
Robert Adams, his sister Barbara
Leighton, her first child Judith,
and Sid Leighton.
*Courtesy of Robert Adams*

John Elden (L) and Robert Adams (R)
at No. 63 Pleasant Street, 1957.
Taken in Bob-a-job week.

# 1. ROBERT ADAMS

Born 9/12/1945 at 57 Gordon Street, Burslem where he lived for 25 years. He married Barbara (nee Steadman) in 1971, then moved to Jackfield Street, adjacent. He now lives in Tunstall.

Date of interview: 24/3/03.

I was born at home, which was 57, Gordon Street, on the Park Estate, Burslem. I still have the doctor's bill and the midwife's bill. There was no National Health Service until 1948, so I was paid for when I was born! My older brother Peter is now 65, and my sister Barbara is 69.

My parents were Percy and Gertrude (nee Goodwin) Adams. Father was a potter's mouldmaker and modeller, and Mother was a guilder, and both worked at Charlton and Thompson's factory in Hanover Street, Burslem[1]. It was a small factory which ceased to operate when the potters first received holiday pay. The owner, Charlie Thompson, was opposed to the idea of paying potters to stop at home. After a few other jobs, Dad joined Wood's Tileries in Ogden Road, off Regent Road, Hanley.

As children we played in the streets on home-made trollies and scooters. We would sometimes drag two pig-bins out into the back entry for wickets when we were playing cricket. I remember rationing ending in the 1950s, and going out to get a Crunchie bar. On the Park Estate where I lived, there must have been forty or fifty small shops including a chemist's, greengrocer's and ironmonger's, but nobody there could sell us a Crunchie bar. Eventually we bought one from Slack's confectionary shop, opposite the Co-op emporium in Queen Street, Burslem. We spent all afternoon trying to get that Crunchie bar.

I recall playing on the coal tip at Sneyd Colliery, doing what we kids called 'mountaineering'. Sneyd Brickworks was off Nile Street[2] and used to extend as far as what we called Cow Lane. There was always lots of coal and rubble, and we'd build 'houses' or 'huts'. You would make a fire and cook spuds, although sometimes we would be chased away by the colliery police.

We would also play on Wade's pottery shraff tip, off the Sytch (Westport Road) where Whimsies could be found, small pottery figures, mainly of animals, which can be bought at collectors' fairs now. All the seconds were thrown on the tips, and we would come home with pockets full of them and give them to mother. They would end up displayed across our mantelpieces[3].

Some of the women on the Park Estate in the 1950s, including my own Mother, would come out in the afternoon after they had done their housework. They'd have their pinafores on, and they would sit either on a little stool or a cushion, on their doorstep, and gossip. Some would smoke, or go in and make a cup of tea. Most had a little back entry, and these were kept spotlessly clean.

The boy who lived next door kept pet rabbits, and on Saturdays, we sometimes went to the joiner's shop at Sneyd Colliery[4] to collect sawdust for them. One weekend, when we were about nine years old, we met two men in the joiner's shop and they asked us if we wanted a job. They told us we would be paid ten shillings a week, and we wouldn't have to go to school any more. They kidded us up! Back home, we told our mothers, and when Dad returned from work, we told him that we'd both left Jackfields school, because we were about to start work in the Sneyd Colliery joiner's shop. We were going to take sandwiches, and a billy-can with tea in it, and make a fire and spit on it, and roast potatoes. We'd got it made!

My father decided to go along with the joke, and when he got home from work the next day, he gave me a clock-card, on which he'd written my name. I was looking forward to 'clocking on' at Sneyd, and I broke my heart when Mother told me that I had to go to school on Monday morning, and that I had to do another six years!

My first school was Jackfield Infants School, which I attended from the age of five. I remember the headmistress, Miss Coxon, and the school's air raid shelters, which were just beginning to be filled in. A supply of coke was tipped near to one of the outside walls, and the boys would run up and down it, playing 'King of the Castle'.

Afterwards, I went to Moorland Road Juniors. However, I never attended the adjacent senior school, as I passed my eleven-plus and joined Stanfields Technical School, whose headmaster was William Potts. I was there from 1957 up to 1962. There was much emphasis on machine-drawing, draughtsmanship, woodwork, metalwork, engineering, plumbing and brickwork. You might describe it as an early college, and eventually it became Stanfields Technical High School.

Mr Jack Berrisford taught machine-drawing or draughtsmanship, and he lived in Bank Hall Road. He was very methodical and particular, and had four turn-ups on his shirt sleeves. He would take a yardstick ruler and walk down the rows of desks, moving the tables so that they were all exactly in line with the ones across and behind. He was strict, and used to hit some pupils with a piece of Bunsen burner rubber tubing. He demanded that we had a half-inch margin on our paper, and when we had a rubber in our hands, we were made to call it art gum. We had to have a 2H pencil sharpened to a chisel point, and all tools had to be laid on our drawing boards just the way he wanted it.

He taught us definitions which would help us to be good draughtsmen, such as *"What is a point? A point has position but no size. Never represent a point by a dot, but merely by the intersection of two lines"*. He would test the boys: *"Adams, what is definition two! Bailey! Definition eight!"*

Years later, I met the teacher in the chip shop in May Street. I said, *"Mr Berrisford, I still remember your definitions, thirty years on!"* He replied that he had begun teaching at the school from 1945, and told me a story about a former pupil who had fought in the Korean War in the early 1950s. At night-time, he had recited the definitions in the trenches in order to cope with the boredom of guard duty.

The school I remember was in two halves. The main building had been the old Haywood Hospital in Moorland Road, but there was an annexe up at High Lane. Because of the walking between the two, and the fact that there was nowhere to put your books, I used to carry two satchels. You might attend one or both schools in a day, depending on your school timetable. It was a six-day timetable, wherein Monday might be Day 1 and

Friday Day 5, but the next Monday would be Day 6, followed by Day 1 again. It was awkward, and some of the children who travelled from far away brought the wrong books.

The old hospital building shut in 1961 and we all relocated to the annexe. There were stairs and corridors which today's health and safety people would certainly oppose. The metalwork room housed belt-driven machinery, so if one person was working on a lathe, about ten lathes would be going at the same time. It seemed ghostly, with no-one operating some of the machines. Up at High Lane you could switch an individual machine off.

At the age of sixteen, I took a job on W.R. Midwinter's Hadderidge Pottery, at the top of Navigation Road, Burslem[5]. The wage was £4 10s. and I left over two years later on £6 10s. I began to learn to be a decorating manager, dealing with on-glaze and underglaze decoration. I had to go to night school on part of what is now the Staffordshire University site, to take a pottery manager's diploma. This was a five-year course from the age of sixteen. You paid your own fees, as Midwinter's wasn't renowned for paying them for you. I would go to work from 8 am until 5.15 pm and on Monday, Wednesday and Thursday evenings I would go home for my books, catch a bus from Burslem to Stoke and attend the course until 9 pm. As a member of staff, I would sometimes go in at weekends for no extra pay, and I knew that some labourers received twice the wage I was on. Also, you had to wait until someone left or died in those days in order to secure a pottery manager's post.

I enjoyed working on Midwinter's but the money was poor. So in 1964 I joined the Michelin tyre plant at Stoke, and was in the quality control department for nearly 38 years.

Notes:
1) Charlton & Thompson Ltd, earthenware manufacturers, Hanover Street, are listed in Kelly's Directory of Staffordshire (1932).
2) Sneyd Brickworks Ltd, Nile Street, is listed in the City of Stoke-on-Trent Directory (1955).
3) Compare this account with that of Wenda Dyer.
4) Sneyd Colliery closed in 1962, the last coal being drawn in July. Its workings had been connected to Wolstanton Colliery, and one of the shafts remained in use for ventilation purposes and also as a second means of egress from the northern end of the Wolstanton workings.
5) Midwinter, W. R. Ltd, Albion and Hadderidge potteries, Burslem, is listed in the City of Stoke-on-Trent Directory (1955).

Sneyd colliery.

Leah Boulton at Royal Doulton, Nile Street, in 1963, painting Toby Jugs.
*Courtesy of Jean Wood.*

## 2. GRAHAM BELL

Born 5/7/1930 in Oakville Avenue, off High Lane, Burslem. He lived there until 1957 when his family moved to Norton. He returned to Burslem in 1990 to live in Moorland Road. He married his wife Irene (nee Meredith) in 1952.

Date of interview: 22/7/2003 and 24/10/2003.

As children, we played by Finney's pond, which was attached to Mr Finney's farm. We built rafts and floated them on the pond. We also walked to Burslem Golf Links. During the war, the Americans played golf on the course, and I remember caddying for them on one occasion. The golf course boasted three ponds on three separate levels, including a large one by the clubhouse at the top. They were a great attraction for us. They teemed with dragonflies and sticklebacks which we used to bring home in jamjars. As the ground fell away, there was a brook which joined two more ponds together.

Sometimes we trespassed on Wilkinson's brickworks[1] at the foot of Acreswood Road. Further on, in Bradeley, the firm had a larger brickworks with tunnel kilns. Wilkinson's narrow gauge railway ran towards the Golf Links, over a footpath, and ended at a marl pit, where they extracted marl.

Near where I lived in Oakville Avenue, there was some spare ground where we used to build six feet square dug-outs, or forts, in the ground. The roof would be constructed of wooden spars and old corrugated iron sheets and then covered over. We would put fireplaces in and spend hours in there roasting potatoes and chestnuts. The inevitable happened - the forts would be raided by other boys. They would jump on them and collapse them.

There would also be 'raids' between local gangs of boys, and our rivals came from Bradeley and Stanfield. Gangs would line up against each other, shout abuse and throw stones at each other. There might be some charging, but there was no close combat.

One game we played was 'bottle tops'. They came from beer bottles, and boys had great collections of these multi-coloured tops. Double Diamond, I recall, was a brilliant yellow with red lettering. There were Parker's brewery tops, too. The idea of the game was that competitors took one of their tops and threw it against a wall, and the owner of the top which landed nearest the wall won that round. He then gathered up all the tops and threw them into the air. The ones which landed face-up, he kept. A game which really caught on.

During the War Years, we had an Anderson shelter delivered to our house in Oakville Avenue. As far as I recall, all houses received one in our locality. Council lorries rolled up and delivered various pieces. The shelters came more or less in kit-form consisting of six curved sheets, a front and back and channel iron for the base. A spanner, nuts and bolts were also supplied. You were given the instruction to dig a cavity for the shelter and then to use the dirt you had excavated to cover the top of the shelter. People say that they were made of corrugated iron, but it was corrugated steel, which was galvanised to prevent rust. My father, Arthur Bell, grew plants over the top of ours, and illuminated the inside with an electric bulb. They didn't leak, but they were prone to flooding on account of natural drainage and accumulating groundwater. We slept in them quite a lot, as my father made bunks. I had two sisters and a brother.

Burslem Auxiliary Fire Service used a pond at Bycars for hose-drills, and my friend and I were allowed to clamber on to the fire engines and travel back to the fire station on High Lane. This was at the rear of a large house occupied at the time by a Mrs Henry Wood. There were outbuildings behind, and a large garage. My friend and I started running errands for the firemen, and they befriended us. There were no health and safety concerns then, and they would take us on their vehicles to different exercises held locally.

I recall Burslem Wakes when they were held in land off Hamil Road, before Port Vale moved there in 1950. Most of this was waste ground, but overlooking Hamil Road were a number of businesses, including Farrington's steel stock holders[2], the Hamil garage, North Staffordshire haulage, the Associated Bus Company[3], Burslem Building Materials[4], and Sambrook's the builder[5]. The land I refer to, to the rear, was known locally as the shawdruck, and potters tipped waste there.

It was later levelled out, and the Wakes held there. Steam traction engines trundled up Hamil Road, towing wagons and rides. Boxing booths were set up, and one year, I saw an ox being roasted. This was later sliced up and sold to the public. I enjoyed watching the attractions being assembled. Burslem Wakes was a big event. Large circuses, such as Chipperfield's used to set up on the same land.

I can understand why Port Vale have experienced occasional subsidence problems, because there were so many pit-shafts on the land. The Associated Bus Company used to tip waste oil down one of them. Some of the shafts were capped but some were reasonably open, only covered by wire netting or barbed wire. Schoolchildren would throw bricks down them and wait for the splash when the bricks hit the water at the bottom.

During my childhood, I recall being bought toys from Hammersley's in St John's Square. Bourne's Sports now occupies the site. It was a departmental store, but it sold brand-name toys such as Hornby, Meccano and Dinky. Even during the War you could acquire a limited supply of Meccano products. Tiley's the chemist stood in Market Place, and they sold Dinky and Meccano products too. One Christmas, I was bought a cinematograph (a type of early film projector) from there. We showed thirty-second films in our air raid shelter.

I also recall Cock's Magnet Drapery Store, which had a large wooden magnet hanging outside. Fred Bewes' shop stood on the site now occupied by an Indian restaurant on the corner of Westport Road. This was an Aladdin's Cave of records, model railways, toys and aeroplane kits. An untidy but interesting place.

I attended Jackfield Infants School, then Moorland Road Junior School. I have quite vivid memories of not being able to go to school until they built the air raid shelters in Lingard Street. We were absent from school for weeks. When they were built, we had air raid drills, and would file into the underground shelters, singing *Roll out the Barrel*. Teachers would stand with a battery lamp, and we sat on wooden forms placed on a concrete floor. Inside the shelters, the smell was not very pleasant at all.

Leah Boulton at her retirement at Royal Doulton, Nile Street, in 1963.
*Courtesy of Jean Wood.*

At the Moorland Road School there was a wooden prefabricated hut building, now long demolished. This was divided up into four classrooms and there was a verandah across the front. They were quite pleasant classrooms. I remember being taught by Miss Jackson in this building. Mr Harrison was the headmaster of the Junior School during my schooldays. The Loopline railway ran along the side of the school, a big attraction for me. At Moorland Road, I recall people giving away the first copy of the Dandy, one lunchtime. This was accompanied by a free gift of some celluloid panpipes. Later on, we received the first Beano in the same way.

Afterwards, I moved to Park Road School, which was my senior school. By this time, the war situation was improving, and so our education began to return to normal. I recall Mr Yeomans, the science teacher, Sidney Cliff who taught music and Mr Lake who was a form teacher who taught art. He was an eccentric. He would drag pupils out of classes, much to the disapproval of some teachers, to take part in the projects he was supervising. He was heavily involved in War Weapons Week, Wings For Victory Week, Warship Week and more. If one of these savings weeks was coming up, he would have us painting murals of battleships or spitfires on the school wall overlooking Hamil Road. Mr Lake was also keen on 'Digging For Victory'. There were allotments in Hamil Road, roughly where the present vicarage is. Pupils tended them, and dug soil over.

This was the role which Mr Lake took on, but I suspect our education suffered in the process. He was also involved in staging school concerts and ran the after-school youth club as well as the school scout troop with Mr Faulkner. I was one of about six or eight children who spent quite a number of Saturday mornings with him, to make up for lost time! He lived in the Milehouse area of Newcastle, and that's where we went for the private tuition. We paid a fee for it, of course, and learned mainly maths.

Mr Grant taught woodwork and was a strict disciplinarian. He wouldn't think twice about hitting you with a piece of wood, or caning boys. Mr Bennett was the headmaster.

The boys and girls at Park Road were taught together in class, but there were separate playgrounds. The boys took woodwork, and the girls domestic science. The sexes were separated for P.E. This was held in the assembly hall, and there were mats and a wooden games horse which could be built up to various heights in sections. All the equipment would just be pushed against the walls in the hall. Our annual sports day took place at Norton cricket ground at Smallthorne. We played football at the bottom of Hamil Road, near where the fire station is now. There were some advertising billboards there, and we played on the small pitch behind them.

At the age of eleven or twelve, I attended drawing classes, one night a week, at the School of Art in Queen Street. The lecturer was Harry Nixon, who was a prominent artist at Royal Doulton's. My friend, Colin Calvert, and I, were the youngest students, the others being adults. The first thing we ever drew was the Burslem coat of arms. Afterwards, it was still life and birds.

During the War, I worked for Berrisford's, the High Lane butcher, as an errand boy. I delivered meat after school and on Saturdays. I had a bicycle with a basket on the front, delivering meat to Milton on Wednesdays, Cobridge on Fridays and in Burslem on

Saturdays. Mr Berrisford also had a stall in the Meat Market[6] behind the Town Hall. This was a stark building, big and cold inside.

I remember the smell of the chlorine at Burslem Baths in Moorland Road. When I was at Park Road School, we held a few swimming galas there. People did daft things, such as hanging off the roof trusses and jumping off the balcony into the pool, which was a regular occurrence. There were no life guards to stop them, although I do recall a caretaker. There was a row of cubicles up each side of the pool. The cubicle doors had space at the bottom and space at the top and there was a small bench at the rear and a few hooks for your clothes. If the baths were in demand at a certain time, there might be three or four children in one cubicle; and if it was really busy, children might go up to the balcony to change.

From about 1937, I began going to the juvenile library at the Wedgwood Institute in Burslem. It was a large library, even for juveniles, as it took all the space up which is now used for selling old books and magazines. On the left hand side on the ground floor was the reading room, where all the daily newspapers, all broadsheets at the time, were laid out on sloping tables. Anyone could go in and read the daily papers. The building was also used as the school of commerce, where office-related subjects and shorthand typing were taught. Notices around the library asked library users to be quiet.

It was a big thing for me to reach the age when I could join the adult library in the Old Town Hall, as we were not a well-off family, and books were a luxury for me. This was a fantastic library, reached by the two staircases which met at the top. There were no empty shelves, and many of them were bound, with titles and authors' names embossed in gold on the covers. The library had a distinctive, musty smell.

I left school at the age of fourteen in 1944. Mother told me that she'd secured a job for me at Boulton's foundry which was otherwise known as William Boulton, Ceramic Engineers[7]. The firm was based on the corner of Navigation Road and Pleasant Street in Burslem. The main entrance was in Pleasant Street. I spoke to Mr Dovey, who told me when I could start. I was paid fourteen shillings per week for 48 hours per week including Saturday mornings. I began a seven year apprenticeship scheme.

In the evenings during my apprenticeship, I was a night school pupil at the Wedgwood Institute. I learnt engineering, maths, drawing and science over several nights a week. The room we used for engineering/maths was a tiered room, in which the pupils could look down towards the lecturer.

I began working in the stores, which was regarded as good grounding, but I was soon transferred to the dies shop, in which dies for tiles were made. During the War, machine gun mountings for tanks were made in there. The company also made castings for gear boxes and military vehicles. For the first year, I was classed as a 'shop lad'. I did errands, brewing tea, lighting stove pots, queuing up in Burslem market for food for the men. I bought whatever food was available, as the War was still on. I also queued for cigarettes for them, and was given instructions: *"Don't come back unless they're Players or Woodbines. Don't buy Pasha!"* I called at tobacconists' and grocers' shops, even going as far as Hanley, as I didn't dare go back without them. The men also sent me for saccharine, to supplement the war time sugar ration, and I went to Boots' in Queen Street for this. It was on the opposite side of the street to its present site.

Another job was preparing the washing up water, every lunchtime and just before the time to go home. Eighteen workers would wash their hands in the bucket of water, though the foreman had a bucket of his own! We prepared the hot water as follows: we inserted blocks of metal into a few of our stove pots, and warmed them up. When they were red hot, we took them out with tongues and placed them in the buckets to heat the water. The men then washed with carbolic soap. When the War was on, there were two twelve hour shifts, but being an apprentice, I wasn't permitted to be rostered in this shift system.

Boulton's was still a family firm when I joined. While Frank Boulton was still alive, all the apprentices were given a half-day holiday on Shrove Tuesday, by the request of William Boulton's will. This came to an end on the death of Frank. As an apprentice centre lathe turner, I worked on the machine gun mountings and then the periscope mountings during the War, but afterwards we reverted to ceramic engineering. This involved making tile presses, but other shops were occupied in other branches of the pottery industry. For instance, there was a sliphouse, a machinery manufacturing shop and a blacksmith's shop.

For meals, workers either took their own sandwiches, or the 'shop lad' fetched chips from Stockton's in Waterloo Road, or another chip shop in St John's Square now occupied by a dry cleaners. There was also a pie shop in Navigation Road, which sold the best pies in Stoke-on-Trent!

In 1945, I joined the air training corps which at the time was based at the old junior technical school in Moorland Road. I was involved on a three-times-a-week basis (including Sunday mornings) until 1949. This was run by the headmaster of Burslem technical school, Mr Collinson. He was commanding officer. We used to parade up and down Moorland Road, and have drill sessions in the school yard. We were involved in the Victory in Europe thanksgiving pageant, and the VJ thanksgiving pageant in the Queen's Hall in Burslem, where all the Wartime voluntary services took part in the show. Parker's Brewery band supplied the music. A spitfire aeroplane was exhibited in St John's Square. We later moved base to Cobridge Barracks and amalgamated with another squadron, commanded by Mr Spendilow, who was a teacher at Moorland Road school. When we first moved to Cobridge, we were given the freedom of the barracks virtually - proper canteen, stores, lecture rooms. However, when the Territorial Army moved in, we were squeezed out into a Nissan hut to the rear.

About halfway through my apprenticeship scheme, I was disenchanted at Boulton's, and so took the chance to join the RAF for National Service in 1949. However, I returned to Boulton's afterwards. I was told that I had been in engineering during my RAF service, and so I could now be set on as a fully-paid journeyman centre lathe turner. The boredom soon returned, though. I was operating a centre lathe one day, machining various components and looking at the whitewashed wall in front of me, and I thought, *"I'm not stopping here for the rest of my life"*. There was continual noise, too. So I found a job at W. Allard, a family firm in Newcastle.

However, I returned to Burslem when I landed a job in the engineering development department at Royal Doulton in 1971. I acted as foreman over the engineering development workshop at the Nile Street plant, and later became project manager at the now-demolished Baddeley Green plant. I retired when I was 61. I enjoyed working at Royal Doulton - certainly until it merged with Allied English Potteries, which was a member of the Pearson Group. I would have to say, though, that I found there was a lot of waste on Doulton's. If there was anything needed, we went out and bought it; we didn't make do with what we'd got. It was a great firm, though, which had its own choir, photography club, art club, and dinghy sailing club. I was involved with the latter for about twelve months in the 1970s. We used Westport Lake. A few of our members had their own boats, and the plan was to purchase some more, but it did not transpire.

Doulton's before the merger embraced the Nile Street plant and others such as Minton's, Dunne Bennett's, and Beswick's, but in my opinion, we lost the personal touch when we merged with Allied English Potteries.

Notes:
1) Wilkinson Brothers (Burslem) Ltd, marl manufacturers, 346, High Lane, Burslem, is listed in Kelly's Directory of Staffordshire (1940).
2) Farrington, J. Arthur & Son, iron merchants, Hamil Road, is listed in Kelly's Directory (1940).
3) Associated Bus Companies Ltd, omnibus proprietors, garage at Hamil Road, listed in Kelly's (1940).
4) (The) Burslem Building Materials Co., builders' merchants, Hamil Road, is in Kelly's (1940).
5) Sambrook (Burslem) Ltd, builders and contractors, plumbers and house decorators, Hamil Road is listed in the City of Stoke-on-Trent Directory (1955).
6) The Meat Market was opened in 1836 and was demolished in 1957-8. The Civic Gardens opened in 1960 to mark the Golden Jubilee of Federation. The Ceramica Shop, opened in 2003, now occupies much of the site.
7) *"Established 1852. William Boulton Limited. Machinery for the manufacture of earthenware, china ware, tiles, electric porcelain and acid jars. Grinding cylinders, disintegrators, etc... Providence Engineering Works, Burslem".* Advert in Kelly's (1940).

Brickhouse Lane.

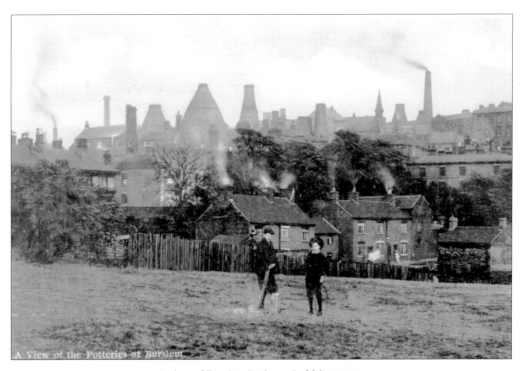

A view of Burslem in the early 20th century.

Swan Bank Wesleyan Methodist chapel.

Cobridge church in the early 20th century.

The Longport Schools being demolished, 18/10/91.

## 3. JOHN BOURNE

Born 4/7/1930 at Freehold Terrace, Middleport (no longer there). He moved to Enoch Street in the early 1950s and to Burmarsh Walk about 1982. As a teenager he worked at Simpson's tileworks in Newport Lane for a year, later becoming a coalminer at Norton and Holditch. Married Stella Mason in 1950.

Date of interview: 15/4/2003.

Freehold Terrace was unusual for a terraced street, as the houses had gardens in front. These backed on to one of the perimeter walls of Middleport Park. On Summer evenings, about six or seven o'clock in the evening, the park was often full. If you didn't get there early, you couldn't get a place on the seats. Families watched the bowlers on the two greens.

Freehold Terrace and Brindley Street ran parallel and there was an entry in between. It was no small one - you could get a waggon down it. People knew it as 'Boulton's entry' on account of the fruiterer's, Boulton's, at the top of the entry. Come bonfire night, bonfires used to be built at the top, middle and bottom of the entry - it was that large an entry.

There must have been thousands of people working in Middleport at places like Malkin's and Simpson's tile factories[1], Wilkinson's pottery, Wood's pottery, the Middleport Pottery of Burgess and Leigh and more.

As a child, I played near the Trent and Mersey Canal, particularly at a spot nicknamed 'Jelly Land'. This was located just beyond Oliver's bridge at the end of Newport Lane. It was an area of spongy grass, and we jumped up and down, bouncing on it. We also played on the shawdrucks at Middleport. When you couldn't afford to go to Burslem public baths, you would swim in the canal on Sunday mornings. I'll be quite honest, it wasn't very nice, because it was the main disposal point for dogs and cats, and I sometimes saw them floating past in bags.

The Burslem Canal (now defunct and drained) was overlooked by the Co-op Bakery, and it virtually ran into Furlong Lane, Burslem. There was a huge basin at the end, and narrow boats would turn around there. There was a massive stabling block, too. Anyone who lived at Middleport at this time will remember the Co-op Bakery horses turning out at about 8 o'clock in the morning. There were probably about 60-80 horses. They would be taken along Newport Lane and then they separated as they reached the main road. Along Newport Lane, there was never any shortage of horse manure for the gardens.

There was a football pitch in the area where McGuinness's scrap merchants is now, and Burslem Albion played there at times. It was not an actual ground, just a pitch on a field with goalposts. I remember that in the 1940s, people would sit on the adjacent embankment to watch the matches.

My first school was Middleport Infants School on the corner of Newport Lane and

Middleport, Longport and Burslem from the top of Pitgreen Lane, Wolstanton in 1928.

Photograph follows on to bottom of opposite page.

Burgess Street and Longport School on Newcastle Street. 'Sports facilities' were basic. The only place where the lads played football was on a patch of land known to Burslem people as 'Corny Eyes' at the bottom of Furlong Lane below the Drill Hall. It was not built on, then, just rough cinders. The boys and their teachers would put their jackets down and play football, here.

Shopping in Middleport was easy. People don't realise how big Middleport was in the 1930s and 1940s. At the top of Wharf Street was the Co-op, and you could get bacon, confectionery and most things there. Opposite the White Swan was the Co-op butcher's. If you did want to shop in Burslem, there was an excellent bus service, run, I think, by Tilstone's. Every quarter of an hour there was a bus from Middleport to Sneyd Green, dropping off outside the Wedgwood Institute in Burslem.

The first pub you came to in Newport Lane was the White Swan, but if you continued along, there was the club on the left hand side, the Moon and Stars[2] on the right, and the Royal Oak[3] at the top of Brindley Street. Next, there was the Potters' Arms[4] at the top of Prospect Street.

In addition to these four pubs on Newport Lane alone, there was the Wharf Tavern[5] in Slater Street. In Wharf Street, there were three pubs on the left hand side: the Port Vale, a Truman's house called the Davenport Arms[6], and the Crewe Arms[7] further below. By Wilkinson's factory was the Bridge Inn[8] which backed on to the Trent and Mersey canal.

I knew the Davenport's Arms well. It had a small bar and a lounge, and you could go upstairs to something of a concert room which you reached by going into the back yard and ascending a flight of steps. Wedding parties were accommodated here. The Royal Oak had a red tiled floor, typical of the time. Nothing fancy, but very clean. There was a big bar counter on your right hand side, and at the top of a short central passage, there was a small outdoor department facing you. There was a snug room on the left, used by numerous old ladies, and just past it, a smoke room.

Many Middleport people remember Georgie King, who had fits. There was no harm in him, but some people were frightened of him. I recall him living at Furlong Lane.

When I first went to live in Enoch Street, about 1950, the churchyard was surrounded by a wall which was then about six feet in height. It was more secluded than it is today. There were gates leading into it. Nearby was the Church Inn[9], a lovely old pub. It was kept by Elsie Clayton, who they used to call the 'quiet woman'. She wasn't quiet, mind - she had a loud voice. She would stand behind the bar with her sleeves up with her arms on the counter. On Sundays in the early 1950s, when it was 12 o'clock opening, I used to sit on my step in Enoch Street, look across the road, and wait for Elsie to open the doors. The pub had a big bar, with the counter on the right hand side curving a little, like a horse shoe. There was also a small snug.

I watched Port Vale at the Old Recreation Ground in Hanley and afterwards at Vale Park. I remember the FA Cup semi-final match between Vale and West Brom at Villa Park, Birmingham, in 1954. Seven trains left from Burslem Station, as well as coaches. I thought I'd take some beer with me, so I bought two large bottles and put them inside my mackintosh. I stood at the rear of the goal at Villa Park, and it was so packed that I couldn't get the beer out of my pockets. At the end of the match, I managed to get them out, and the beer was warm as tea!

Notes:

(1) Simpson, T. A. and Co. Ltd, enamelled tile makers, Newport Lane, is listed in Kelly's (1940).

(2) The Moon and Stars P.H., at 118, Newport Lane, kept by Cornelius Machin, Kelly's (1940).

(3) The Royal Oak is listed in the Potteries and Newcastle Directory (1912) as a beerhouse in Newport Lane, proprietor W. H. Plimbley.

(4) The Potters Arms, at 186, Newport Lane, kept by Leonard T. Milner, in Kelly's (1940).

(5) The Wharf Tavern, at 12, Slater Street, kept by Mrs. Eliz. Walker, in Kelly's (1940).

(6) The Davenport Arms stood on the corner of Wharf Street and Hitchin Street and was owned by Messrs. Truman, Hanbury and Buxton & Co. Ltd, brewers of Burton-on-Trent. Plans for the pub, dated 1953, indicate that there were three smoke rooms and a public bar on the ground floor, as well as a central passage. John recalls the upstairs club room which was indeed reached by an external staircase.

(7) The Crewe Arms stood on the corner of Wharf Street and Daniels Street.

(8) The Bridge Inn appears as a beerhouse in the 1912 directory. It was kept by Mary J. Holdam and was situated in West Street, Middleport.

(9) The Church Inn, 1, Enoch Street, proprietor Corbet Reynolds, in the 1912 directory.

Bowling Green at Middleport Park.

A further picture of the Longport Schools in the process of demolition, 18/10/91.

## 4. WENDA DYER

Born Wenda Holt, 12/19/1946 at the Limes Hospital, Hartshill. She was adopted and grew up with her stepfather; her maiden name Zwolinska. She lived at Furlong Lane in Burslem from 1953 until she joined Madeley College in 1965. She is now a teacher at Thistley Hough High School in Penkhull.

Date of interview: 2/12/2003.

Before the Clean Air Acts, the smoky atmosphere of local industry created what were virtually 'pea-soupers' in Furlong Lane. All the houses had cellars, and big front rooms with bay windows. There was a scullery behind the kitchen. Down the back yard there was a toilet with an area for your ashes next to it. The dustbin men came up the narrow entry to the rear. As children, we played at 'Corny Eyes'[1] nearby, where there were two sets of swings.

I attended Hill Top primary school.[2] I remember the rooms being cold, at least until the janitor had fed the boilers with coal. The teachers had been there for a long time, and there was a good atmosphere. There were two bomb shelters, one in the middle of the playground and another at the top end. P.E. equipment was kept in one of them, and the other was full of dirt.

The headmaster at the time was Mr Young. One day, he asked me and a fellow pupil, John Durber, to fetch some important papers from his house in Hanford, where we met his wife. John and I travelled by bus to and from Hanford, and it seemed to take for ever.

The teachers had speciality areas, but taught general subjects. I recall Mr. Hill, who was my second year teacher, who taught P.E. to the boys. He was my favourite teacher, as he taught me long division with recurring numbers when I was eight. I enjoyed helping him with the register at the end of the year, when there was lots of long division to be done. In my third year, Mrs Colclough taught crafts and basket weaving.

In the fourth year, my teacher was Miss Fenton who eventually married a Mr Kilgariff and moved to Walsall. I took a collection for her to buy her a wedding present. She took the girls for P.E., but she was also very artistic. She created a history timeline drawing, which featured our own illustrations. When we were studying countries from around the world, and she would draw children in their national clothing which we would colour in. These were later displayed in the school corridors.

I had to repeat my fourth year, as I was still too young to go to Brownhills Girls School, and so Miss Farmer was my teacher in my final year. She mainly taught music, but other subjects too. Other teachers I remember include Mr. Whalley, who taught ceramics, or clay work. I made a mug which was cut out of rolled-out clay. It was coated with blue slip, and was very wonky, but my mother kept it for a long time.

There was also Mr Sylvester, who would take us to Hanley Museum in Pall Mall for a lecture. I was in the class from Hill Top which used to walk from the school to North Road School in Cobridge and listen to the music being played by sections of the Halle Orchestra in the school hall. Sometimes, the woodwind section would come, or

This photograph from the early 20th century shows the Vine on the corner of Hamil Road and Moorland Road, Burslem. It was later demolished and rebuilt further along Hamil Road.

Harold Harper and Brian Moston at Smith & Moston Tiled Fireplaces, on Newcastle Street and Westport Road, Burslem. (26/2/02)

sometimes the percussion section or the string section, and they would play in the school hall. Pupils from other schools attended, too.

There was an annual school sports day, held at Cobridge Stadium. This embraced sack races, 100 yards relay and long jumping and high jumping. There were four 'houses' - red, yellow, green and blue. There were captains in the fourth year, and I was the red house captain. The team with the most points for the year received a plaque to keep for twelve months. Shields used to be given each Monday to whichever house had the best attendance in the previous week. These were displayed on a large board in the school hall. The cane was used at Hill Top, but I never received it. I was probably one of the pupils who never got caught!

When I was in the top class at Hill Top, we were sometimes given guided tours around the Wade's factory and met the pressers and other operatives. We were given milk and biscuits and before we left, we were each given a small box of Wade Whimsies. I still have the Jungle set, the Farm set and the Hunt set. They do not sell them in the boxes anymore. I used to play on the top of Wade's shraff tip, and once found a plate with a huge sunflower design on it. My father hated eating off it, as he disliked the flower appearing through his food.

My friends and I sometimes went 'ratting' among the shraff in the Westport Lake area, to the rear of Price and Kensington's pottery in Longport. We would throw rocks at the rats. We also played on the Grange pond in Cobridge. I caught newts and small fish. We made lead soldiers there, by melting lead in a tin can suspended over a fire. The lead would then be poured into moulds.

In the early 1960s, I worked at Christmas, plucking pheasants' feathers for Tom Slack, whose fruit and vegetable shop was in Queen Street[3]. This enabled me to earn money for Christmas. I left Hill Top to go to Brownhills School, but I still walked past Hill Top en route every day, passing Wade's shraff tips on my way down the Sytch.

I used to swim at Burslem Baths in Moorland Road on several nights a week. You entered through turnstiles just inside the door and paid your money. Once you had proved that you could swim a length of the pool, you were given a half-price ticket. There was a large and a small pool, and a slipper bath which was often used by miners and their families, especially on Friday nights. This pool was large enough to swim in. The miners would emerge a completely different colour.

During the polio outbreak, around 1957, they increased the chlorine content of the water and this was agony on the eyes. You would go home almost blind, with your eyes streaming, seeing haloes around the street-lamps. We were not supposed to run about around the pool, but we did anyway, playing 'tag'. We would also bomb into the water. There was also the Turkish baths, superintended by Mrs Higginson.

After we had finished our swimming session, we would play water polo - often, it was girls versus boys. There were no facilities for drying your hair, and you had to do it with your towel. I always went home with my hair wet.

Other girls and myself were trained by Derek Taylor. He was an absolute slave-driver, but with good intentions. He had a really good swimming team. He took me to the All-England competition in Grimsby. Mrs Higginson went along as my chaperone, as well as Derek's wife and daughter. We all travelled in his Morris Minor.

Among the businesses in Burslem, I recall the Chinese laundry to the rear of Woolworth's. This was run by the Yee family. I also recall Hammersley's shop in St. John's Square. Mother bought needles and threads from there. Just inside the Covered Market off Queen Street, there was a toy stall, the first stall on the right. My brother bought me a tiny, five-inch teddy bear as a Christmas present from this outlet. The head turned, and its arms and legs moved.

At Askey's fish shop, all the fish were on ice. The game would be hanging up - rabbit, grouse, pheasant. Game pie which included venison was also sold. On one occasion, I bought a bag of mixed game from Askey's, and I made a game pie. Mother wouldn't eat it, but I loved it.

A friend and I used to sneak into the Art School when the life models were posing for the students who were doing figure-drawing. It was easily done. We'd just go up the stairs, looking out for anyone coming and peek into the room through the window panes in the doors.

As a girl of eighteen or nineteen, I would visit the George Hotel on Sunday evenings with my friends, and we would dance. I recall dancing to *Help!* by the Beatles[4], with Nicky Machin from Smallthorne. There was a ballroom with a wooden floor and this was very popular with the 18-24 age group. It was a nice way of socialising, contemporary music from the hit parade being played for dancers. Patrons dressed well, many of them wearing suits. Mother made me special clothes which I often wore on Sunday.

Notes:
1) Compare this account of 'Corny Eyes' with that of John Bourne.
2) Hill Top school was demolished in 2003.
3) Samuel Slack, greengrocer (No. 7) and confectioner (No.11) Queen Street, in Kelly's (1940).
4) *Help!* entered the hit parade on July 29 1965, and was a number one hit for the Beatles.

The marl pit at Cobridge c 1920.

The Moorcroft Pottery c 1950.

Outside St Joseph's Catholic Church, Hall Street, looking towards the sides and rear of the Hilltop Methodist Chapel. C.1980. *Courtesy of Harold Gordon.*

## 5. EILEEN ELLIS

Born Eileen Frain, 4/8/1933 at 25, Broad Street (later Evans Street), Burslem. She lived at Hanover Street for about six months; at the Liberal Club in Market Place from circa 1933 to 1938; at Burnhayes Road (off Scotia Road) for a year; then into Edge Street in December 1939. She was one of seven children, the last born in 1947. She married at St Joseph's Catholic church in Burslem in 1956, and then went to live in Hanley. She worked in Tunstall. She came back to live in Burslem, at Park Road, in 1979.

Date of interview: 21/5/2003.

I attended St Joseph's Catholic school in Hall Street, from the age of four to fifteen. I recall Miss Steele (who later married and became Mrs Bickerton), who was a music teacher. She would hit you on top of the head with a ruler if she saw you miming in class, rather than singing properly. I had the cane once for talking and giggling in church.

I should have left at the age of fourteen, but in that year, the school leaving age was raised to fifteen. I had wanted to leave in order to earn some money, but the last year was brilliant. We were taken to youth hostels, and we had a very laid-back teacher, Mr Reg Foskett, who had recently come out of the army. I remember how the headmaster had introduced him to us, just before our last year. He was wearing army uniform, and carrying a stick under his arm. He had evidently been a teacher before he went into the forces. He taught us how to dance, and allowed us girls to attend school in our 'curlers'. If you misbehaved, he would make you take one of your 'curlers' out so that a wisp of your hair flopped down. I don't think the school was really prepared, or had the equipment for the fifteen-year-olds, and the concert room became a makeshift room for our class.

The pupils in my year would receive benediction on a Sunday night, and afterwards, Mr. Foskett and his wife would teach children how to dance in an upstairs classroom of the school. He would also take us to orchestral concerts at the Victoria Hall, Hanley. Brown's dance hall stood nearby in Hall Street, and I often went there on a Tuesday night. It was like a large hut or a glorified barn, run by a husband and wife. Both were brilliant dancers, and they would teach dancing. I remember what we called the 'kissing waltz': a chap would ask you to dance a last waltz, and he'd give you a kiss on the cheek at the end. I never went after about 1948.

As children in Edge Street, we would attach long pieces of string to tin cans and then walk on them, as if they were stilts. We would also play 'rosy apple', and go to certain houses where we knew the owner would 'run' us. Tilstone's bus garage was nearby, overlooking Scotia Road. We would play in there, and sometimes they didn't secure the buses and we would actually play in them, before being 'run off'. The garage building is still there.

When we played rounders in Edge Street, we occasionally broke windows in houses. Edge Street was a cul-de-sac, and shaped like a lollipop. At the top, was a gas lamp, which we would use as a wicket for cricket. If we broke someone's window with a ball, our parents would have to club together to pay for it, and they would take this out of our pocket-money. Many of the houses had perhaps fifteen or twenty feet of gardens in front with a fence at the bottom. When we played cricket, the idea was basically to hit shots down the street, and if the ball went into someone's yard, you were 'out'. Some neighbours wouldn't give you the ball back.

Between Chatterley Street and Westport Road there were numerous allotments. During wartime rationing, we would pinch turnips and carrots from there, and eat them. My mother had a trick for making butter. She would take the cream off the top of a bottle of milk and put it in a jar. We would then sit and shake it until it turned to butter. Even then, it tasted horrible and sour. We also ate lard on toast, sometimes salted.

When there were air raids and we were at school, we pupils would be marched out to the bottom of the yard and taken into a brick shelter near Spens Street. There were doors at each end, and no windows. They used to put flags or paving stones on top of some of these shelters, presumably to disguise them from the air. We had an Anderson shelter in our back garden, but our next-door-but-one neighbour, Mrs Hulme, had a 'posh' one, with a carpet in. Ours had seats in, but water always accumulated in it. More often than not, we'd hide under a table, or in our pantry! On V. E. Day, there was a street party in Edge Street. Mother dragged our piano out on to the top step outside our door, and played it in full view of the street.

I helped out in my friend's parents' chip shop (long disappeared) across from the police station in Jackson Street. It was kept by Sheila Edwards' family. This would have been during my last year at school. We used to work in the cellar below, with a big tub of potatoes which had gone through a primitive automatic rotating peeler. We would then have to get the 'eyeholes' out, and would then receive some money for the pictures as a reward.

As a teenager, I watched some brilliant bands at the Queen's Hall in Burslem. On Friday nights, at certain times of the year, factory dances were held there. They tended to be all-ticket. The Saturday night dances were very popular, especially when Reg Bassett's band were playing. Before there was a bar, there was a 'pass out' ticket which would allow you to exit during intervals in the band music, and go for a drink at the Roebuck pub opposite.

In 1955, our house in Edge Street became one of the first houses around Scotia Road to boast a rented television. It was a Rediffusion television, and as we were a big family with lots of friends, people used to come around to watch it.

I shopped for clothes at Cock's, which was a large shop in Market Place, and Hammersley's, where Bourne's Sports in St John's Square is to be found now. I remember the smell of Boyce Adams's, a lovely shop, which is where Burslem Post Office is now. There was sawdust on the floor, and you could get some nice cakes there in the late 1950s. Victor Kent's was a gents' outfitters shop in Market Place, but we couldn't afford his clothes. He used to stand outside the shop, just like a tailor's dummy, with his white hair and immaculate dress sense.

Notes:
1) Victor Kent, gents' outfitter, 44, Market Place, is listed in Kelly's (1940).

Newcastle Street, Dale Hall,
early 20th century.

The 'New' Market.

The Foaming Quart, Greenhead Street, Burslem.  Date unknown.

Queen Street and the Star public house.

## 6. BERNARD FRAIN

Born 9/6/1931 at 25, Broad Street (later Evans Street), Burslem. He lived at Hanover Street for about six months; at the Liberal Club in Market Place from circa 1933 to 1938; at Burnhayes Road (off Scotia Road) for a year; then into Edge Street in December 1939. He moved to Evans Street when he married in 1961 and lived there until 2000. A bricklayer by trade, he helped with the footings for the new Swan Bank Methodist Church, around 1970. He was employed by Elsby Brothers at the time. He still lives in Burslem.

Date of interview: 7/4/2003.

My only school was St Joseph's Catholic School in Burslem which I attended from the age of 4 to the age of 14, through from infants and juniors to the seniors. I reached the school via Packhorse Lane, and walked past Alcock's cycle shop[1], on its corner site, past Lycett's shop[2] which sold blinds, Willett's foundry (to the rear of the Co-op), and then the school gates. Just further down was Ford's potbank[3], which overlooked our school.

In the Infants school, I recall Sister Bernard. In the afternoon about 2 o'clock, you'd have a little sleep on a canvas bed. Miss Devenport taught in the Junior school, as did Miss Steele, Mrs Moran and Mrs Kelly. In the senior school, there was a teacher called Dermot O'Riley. Discipline was strict. You were caned on the hand for fighting, or throwing ink pellets, and if you were late you were given a verbal warning, followed by a second if necessary, and then the 'stick' if you were late three times in the same week.

There was nothing wasted, in terms of school paper. If paper was used on one side, it would be saved, and then essays could be written on the reverse. Even after that, the paper was saved and mashed up for papier mache sculptures. It being a Catholic school, it didn't have the grants which some other schools enjoyed, and parents paid for quite a few items. We used inkwells, and pencils with a wooden shaft with a nib on the end.

After registration, at 9.30 a.m., we took religious instruction for about ten minutes, followed by other lessons. When Father Browne came round to examine the classrooms, all the canes were removed from sight by the teachers, although sometimes, he would tap you across the back of the legs. He would walk around during your afternoon break, and you would sometimes feel the tap of a stick on your calves. We wore short trousers, of course. He might say, *"Hello, Frain, what mass were you at on Sunday?"* There were three or four masses, and if you hadn't been to church, you always found out on Monday morning what mass Father Browne had taken. So you would answer that you'd attended one of the masses not taken by him!

At playtime we usually had a third of a bottle of milk each, then we would play in the yard for a while. We had an hour and a half for lunch, and some children went home, as I did. However, if you were eligible, you could visit the dinner centre in Church Street (now William Clowes Street). You could have a free lunch there. All denominations went there, including children from Moorland Road or Hill Top school. The building is

The caption of this cigarette card, courtesy of John Booth, is:
Port Vale FC: This club formed 50 years ago plays in Division III (Northern section) of the league
L-R, back row: H. Pinkerton, G. Shenton, J. Baker, F. Malbon, M. Curley, J. Vickers
2nd row from back: T. Holford (trainer), H. Griffiths, K. Gunn, J. Bewick, C. Birks, J. Potts, M. Wilson, H. Tooton (Asst. Trainer)
2nd row from front: G. Glidden, W. Rhodes, G. Stabb, L. Dean, A. Cauldwell
Front row: F. Mitcheson, R. Jones (capt), R. Welsh, H. Dackins.

no longer there, and neither is Hanover Street, which ran to the rear.

I remember a school trip to Sneyd Colliery in 1945, and we went down the pit for a brief tour. There were also a couple of visits to the Victoria Hall in Hanley, and I saw the Liverpool Philharmonic Orchestra.

As children, we would sometimes trespass on to Wade's potbank along Greenhead Street. There were stacks and stacks of cocoa and coffee beans being stored on the premises, this being Wartime, and we would sneak in and get some. The old wooden Hippodrome theatre, (the 'Blood Tub') which used to stand opposite Barratt's manufactory, was also full of coffee beans. We would steal in, and swing across the stage on hanging ropes. The theatre stood derelict until being demolished after the War[4].

Our family shopped at the Co-op in Newcastle Street, but during the time my father, James Edward Frain, was the steward at the Liberal Club in Market Place, we patronised the Maypole grocery store[5] across the road. There was no alcohol sold at the club, but tea, coffee, sandwiches and toasted cheese were available for the members, many of whom were solicitors. My mother Gladys used to make sandwiches for them, and I would run across the road to fetch butter or cheese. There were three full-size billiard tables in the club. Part and parcel of Mother's job was to clean the offices which were used by the professional people who used the same building. It was a three-story building and we lived at the rear of the top story.

There were two entrances to the Palladium cinema[6], one in Cleveland Street, the other in Waterloo Road. Next door was the New Palace which became the New Ritz in 1951, and across the road, the Coliseum. I thought that whilst the Palace was tight for leg-room, the 'Col' was different. It was luxurious, especially upstairs, or if you were in the boxes at the back.

In the late 1940s and early 1950s, a group of us would meet at the Foaming Quart in Greenhead Street on Saturday nights. If we then decided to go to the Queen's Hall that evening, one of us would go to the hall to buy the tickets, and we would ask for a 'pass out'. This meant that you had to be back at the Queen's for 9.50 pm, and if you weren't, you couldn't get in. The point of buying the tickets early was to ensure that you could go drinking around the town first, and then still get into the Queen's later on. If you were later than 9.50 pm., there was no way you could get in because there was a policeman on the entrance as well as the doorkeeper. The policeman eyed people up, and if he thought you were too drunk, he wouldn't let you in. Nobody argued, as the police station was only to the rear, in Jackson Street. Once inside, you would find the bar upstairs open until half past ten. There were no draught drinks available, only bottled beer. You were not allowed to bring drinks downstairs. You could sit at the side of the dance floor with a glass of lemonade, as the girls did, but you couldn't walk around with a beer in your hand. There were chairs around the dance floor, or you could watch from the balcony upstairs. Big bands led by Ken Griffiths, Norman Jones and Ken Bassett used to perform at the Queen's. These were often fifteen or sixteen piece bands, perhaps with three singers in each.

If you had a fish and chip supper afterwards, you would go to two shops on the left hand side of Waterloo Road going towards Hanley and just past the traffic lights. Alcock's and Stockton's were just a few doors away from each other. You would visit the one with the shortest queue. Fish, chips, peas, bread and butter and a cup of tea would cost about one shilling and eightpence, and at either shop you could eat upstairs or down or take your meal away.

Some pubs had certain reputations at the time. The Duke William was regarded as a bit posh, and so was the Leopard. We used to use the public bar (now it is the Stitch In Time premises). I learned to play darts there, in a small alcove which was reached by a couple of steps. The present bar room was the 'best bar', and we didn't think about going in there at our age, because it was always a penny or twopence extra. Near the bottom of the stairs in the Leopard was a desk often manned by a receptionist. The present lounge on the right hand side of the pub was once two rooms, and you sat and pressed a bell-push for service. You would then be served by a waiter. Before going to the Queen's we would use pubs such as Ye Olde Crown, the White Hart (now the Huntsman) or the Mason's Arms. I always loved the Star, in Queen Street, which many people said was a rough pub. It always had an atmosphere. People talked to you and you could play cards or skittles. Yes, it was well-worn and there was no plush seating, but it was a good pub.

In the early 1950s, Jimmy Leigh was the publican at the 'Jig Post', the proper name of which was the Royal Express, on Bourne's Bank[7]. He was a small bloke with a slight limp, with very short hair and spectacles. His brother, Frank Leigh, was a scaffolder who worked as a barman at the Mason's Arms in St John's Square. The Jig Post was just below the Palace and the Coliseum, and so if you were queuing for the pictures and it started to rain, a lot of people would say, *"We'll go [to] the pictures tomorrow night - we'll go and have a pint instead"*.

There were occasions when you entered the pub, and Jimmy would be cutting peoples' hair in the smoke room. The smoke room was on the left, and the bar on the right. His wife would serve behind the bar whilst he gave chaps a five-minute short back and sides. I often saw him do this, and he'd cut pensioners' hair for less money than they'd pay at the barbers. It was a pub known to the 'shilling women' who'd stand in the drinking passage with half a pint. To the rear of the pub was the Ladies', the Gents' and a long yard which was dark down the bottom end. The women took men down there, and the 'Jig Post' was noted for this in the late Forties and early Fifties. Sometimes, businessmen would pick up prostitutes in the pub - not openly, but there'd be a nod and a wink to make the arrangement.

A well-remembered character was Georgie King, who appeared to suffer from an affliction. He was a tall chap who would walk along a pavement, with his head up. He'd suddenly stop and begin to stagger backwards for a few yards. Then he would recover, straighten, and carry on before he was stricken again. Georgie often used Rawlin's Café adjacent to the Old Town Hall in Market Place. The bus drivers who had parked behind the Town Hall when they were en route for Chesterton and Silverdale via Burslem, had their meal breaks from the café. They would brew up at the café, and then drink their tea and eat on their parked buses, the conductors talking to the drivers. Many of them would buy or give George something to eat. He was something of a loner who wore a trilby and a long coat.

My earliest football memory was of my father taking me down to the Victoria Ground, Stoke, around 1942. Stan Matthews was playing for the RAF against the Army. Dad said, *"Now you've seen the finest outside-right you'll ever see playing football"*. A short while after, he took me to the Old Recreation Ground in Hanley to see Port Vale. He told me, *"You've seen Matthews, now you can watch one of the finest inside forwards you will ever see"*. I replied, *"Who's that, Dad?"* He said, *"I'm not telling you, but he's got red hair and you'll see him run out of the tunnel in a minute"*. It turned out to be the Irish international, Peter Doherty, who was guesting for Port Vale, it being Wartime[8].

I used to watch Vale and Stoke on alternative weekends - Vale only from the late 1950s. I got to know players such as Terry Miles, Tommy Cheadle[9], Roy Sproson and Colin Askey, many of whom went to the Vale Café after training. Others such as Basil Haywood, Stan Turner and Ken Griffiths would like to have a game of snooker in the still-standing snooker hall, before catching the bus home.

Notes:
1) Alcock's, radio dealers, Market Place & office and warehouse, Liverpool Road, Kelly's (1940).
2) Lycett's, window blind makers, Market Place, is listed in Kelly's (1940).
3) Ford and Sons Ltd, earthenware manufacturers, Newcastle Street, in Kelly's (1940).
4) According to the Victoria County History, the Hippodrome theatre (the 'Blood Tub') was "the home of popular variety" in the inter-war years, thanks to the direction of Pat Collins, the fairground entrepreneur (d.1943). The venue closed by 1940 and was demolished in 1947-8.
5) The Maypole Dairy Company Ltd, butter dealers, Market Place, is listed in Kelly's (1940).
6) The Palladium Cinema opened as the Burslem Cinema Theatre in 1910, becoming known as the Palladium by the 1920s. It closed in the early 1940s and was subsequently used as a health food shop. The Burslem Picture Palace in Cleveland Street, a converted skating rink, opened in 1911. This was the theatre which in 1936, suffered a roof collapse, following a heavy snowfall. Fortunately, it had not opened that day, as a mark of respect to King George V, who had died the previous evening. Following demolition, the building reopened as the New Palace on October 1, 1936. It later became the Ritz and then the Essoldo before becoming a bingo hall in the 1960s. It was demolished in 1989. The Coliseum opened as a picture theatre in the 1920s, having originally been a music hall. It closed in 1960 as the Gaumont.
7) The Royal Express later became the Unity Club and later, the Summerhouse Club until 1995. It now stands derelict (2004).
8) Doherty played two games for Vale, against Notts County (away) and in the return, at the Old Recreation Ground. Bernard recalls the home game on October 28th 1944 [Source: *The Port Vale Record 1879-1993* by Jeff Kent].
9) The Port Vale FC pub was renamed Tommy Cheadle's in 2003 to commemorate the 50th anniversary of the Vale v. Aston Villa FA Cup semi-final, and Cheadle's accomplishments as captain of the team. Cheadle joined Vale in 1946, and stayed until 1957.

The early Haywood Hospital c.1910.

High Lane in the early 20th century.

## 7. JOAN FRANCE

Born Joan Hudson, 24/3/1928 in Hill Street, Burslem. She has also lived in Murhall Street, Burslem, as well as addresses in the Wolstanton area. She was educated at Cobridge church school between the ages of four and nine, and recalls that the headmaster, Wilf Kirkham, once played football for Port Vale. She also attended schools in Wolstanton. She married Bill France in 1952, at the Bethel chapel in Waterloo Road.

Date of interview: 5/8/2003.

My aunt, Hannah Hudson, was a dressmaker, so she very often shopped at Cock's in Market Place, Burslem, when I was growing up in the Thirties. This was a big shop which was a general drapery store, selling mainly ladies' clothes, curtain material, rugs, dress material, hats, gloves and haberdashery. It was quite a busy store, with Cock's entry to one side. The name of Cock's appeared on the shop's bags.

I also recall the Covered Market off Queen Street from this time. I always looked around Peacock's stall which sold toys and other items. Also in the Covered Market was Pointon's, which sold flowers and things like tomatoes. My father worked on their stall. Slack's used to sell 'shilling dinners' - a skinned rabbit and a few vegetables to go with it. Their stall was near one of the entrance doors as you came in off Queen Street. Two of the Stockton brothers had stalls in the market, and Frank Stockton kept a shop in Waterloo Road.

I had been christened at Bethel Methodist chapel and our family were staunch chapel goers. I went to the Sunday school there, on Sunday mornings and afternoons, and also to the youth club. I started in a toddlers' class. My parents expected me to go, and I enjoyed it. Our Sunday school clothes were only worn on the Sabbath, and we had to put them away and keep them clean when we returned home. My parents would not let us spend any money on Sundays, and we were not allowed to play outside - only in the house. We played games and read books, and our parents left us to find our own amusement. You have to remember that by the time you had been to Sunday school twice, and had your meals, there was not a great deal of spare time left.

In our early days at the Sunday school, we carried 'star cards', and every time you attended, you had a star placed on them. I earned books for good attendance, including *Little Women* by Louisa May Alcott. I also received a Bible, at the front of which was a label indicating that it had been presented to me. When our family moved to Wolstanton, Mother sent me to May Bank Methodist Sunday school, but I didn't like it, as I was so used to the Bethel. So I would often travel on the bus to Burslem, attend lessons at the Bethel, stay at my aunt's house for tea, and then return home.

One of the teachers was Miss Beeston. She was very strict, and would suffer no messing about by her pupils. She often had us singing in class, and liked the singing of hymns. Her brother Fred kept a furniture shop on Waterloo Road and was a Methodist Circuit preacher. In an age when very few people owned motor cars, he had one, and the

The Wedgwood Institute.

Louise Street in the early 20th century.

Beeston family would go out to the countryside in it.

The Sunday School Anniversary took place at the beginning of May, and saw us walking around the streets off Waterloo Road, such as Wellington Street, Stonely Street and Pitt Street. They liked you to have a white dress for the Anniversary, and my aunt used to make a few clothes for us.

At the age of around sixteen, you were asked if you would become a member of the Methodist church, and I joined at that age. I was given a membership certificate, and was also asked if I would join the chapel choir. I did. Sometimes, we would have choir outings to the seaside, or out into the country. This was a friendly get-together, mainly involving choir members. We would sing whilst travelling on the coach. Some of the men in the choir were hilarious, and we would have a really good time on these trips. People such as Eddie Stanley and his brother Cyril, Billy Goodwin and Tom Reynolds used to help to stage concerts, and do silly things such as dress up as women. We used to have an annual sale of work, which would take place on a Saturday. My aunt and other people used to make items to sell on stalls in order to raise money for the chapel. The concerts would then take place in the evening. There was an admission price, and they were well-attended by chapel people.

I recall singing "I'm H-A-P-P-Y" at the chapel, and we would also sing a number of anthems, which were rehearsed during one night in the week. I remember that Mr Pickin was the choirmaster, and he was later replaced by Jim Palmer, who had been a long-serving Bethel member. He had played the piano there, and worked for Barnett's printers near to St. John's church.

I went to work at A. P. Tiley's chemist[1] in Market Place, Burslem, when I was 21. I had been working at Brown's chemist's in Fenton, but I applied for the job in Burslem because the travelling to work was getting me down. Whilst I was working at Tiley's, Cock's was still trading. I remember old Mr Cock walking up and down his shop. If he saw any children, he gave them sweets. On the right hand side of the shop was Cock's entry, then a mens' clothes shop, owned by Boult's[2] (later Hayden's), then Pidduck and Beardmore's ironmongers[3], and then the Marquis of Granby pub (now the Saggar Makers).

Then there was a covered entry with a gate, between the pub and Tiley's. Lunn Poly, the travel agency, is where Tiley's was. Tiley's was an old-fashioned chemist's with pull-out drawers in the shop and rows of bottles. Mr Tiley was only there for limited hours, but he was helped by Mr Ernest George, who knew many people in Burslem. He was a qualified chemist and managed the shop. As a dispensing assistant, I helped with prescriptions, working there for about ten years. Customers would come to us and ask what we could give them to cure their colds. Mr. George would make suggestions, but he would tell them: *"You've come here without anything on your head"*. They would reply, *"Well, I've only walked a few yards"*. He would say, *"It doesn't matter how many yards you've come. You should have something on your head, because that's how you catch colds"*. Mr George was quite old-fashioned, and he firmly believed that the customer was always right. Mr Tiley himself made us tremble a bit, and I used to try and keep out of his way.

Swan Bank Methodist Church in the 1960s. *Courtesy of Eric Sherratt.*

Leicester's[4] chemist stood opposite ours, and is now Wade's pottery shop. There was also Charles's[5] chemist in Queen Street, as well as Boots'. It was often the case that we only kept small quantities of some of the drugs, as we wanted them to stay fresh. On occasions, someone would come in with a prescription only to find that we had run out of the medication. In these cases, we would borrow from other chemist's. We would write down on a piece of paper what we wished to borrow, and then ask for it from elsewhere. When you next had it in stock, you would return what you had borrowed.

The different chemist shops provided a service to the public by which one would remain open when the other traders in Burslem were closed - for example, during half-day closing, or on Sundays. Prescriptions would be dispensed to people who had visited the doctor's. Nowadays, chemists tend to have drugs already made up. However, when I worked at Tiley's, I would have to make up bottles of mixtures, and I even made up pills and tablets. We had a hand-operated pill-making machine, and I last saw one of these at the Black Country Museum in Dudley, about three years ago. You made a mixture from the constituents, and rolled it until you had a long strip of it. The machine's purpose was to cut the strip up into pill-shapes for customers. Sometimes, I did not finish at Tiley's until 7.30 pm on Saturday evenings. However, if I finished earlier, my future husband Bill and I would visit a chip shop in St. John's Square.

After we had eaten we would often join the queues in Bourne's Bank for the Coliseum cinema. Sometimes, they would let you in, on a 'standing room only' basis, and you could go into the auditorium when there was a spare seat. Of course, the film may have been halfway through by the time we got in, but this was accepted. The films were on a continuous loop, and you could see the same film twice over if you wished to.

When Bill and I were first married, we purchased our meat every week from the Meat Market in Market Place. The stalls were always kept clean, and there was sawdust on the floor. Shortly after we were married, the Bethel chapel closed. Members were transferred to other chapels, normally close to where they lived. We were transferred to Swan Bank Methodist chapel (which was later rebuilt) as it was the nearest to us. We never took to it. We knew very few people there, and I didn't feel comfortable.

Notes:
1) Tiley, Arth. Percvl., dispensing chemist, 35, Market Place and 24, Dartmouth Street, is listed in Kelly's (1940).
2) Boult, Alfred, tailor, 27, Market Place, is listed in Kelly's (1940).
3) Pidduck and Beardmore Ltd, ironmongers, 29, Market Place, is listed in Kelly's (1940).
4) Leicester's (Burslem) chemists and druggists, 38 Market Place and manufacturing chemists, Murhall Street, is mentioned in Kelly's (1940).
5) Charles, Thos., chemist and druggist, 38, Queen Street, is listed in Kelly's (1940).

Queen Street in the early 20th century.

In this chapter is a series of images from the filming of *The Card* (from the Arnold Bennett book) in 1951, showing Middleport. Alec Guinness was the starring actor. *Courtesy of Harold Gordon.*

Filming of *The Card*, showing Middleport in 1951. *Courtesy of Harold Gordon.*

## 8. HAROLD GORDON

Born 20/6/1927 at 46, Navigation Street, which faces Middleport Park; his mother Lily (nee Pennington) had been born next door at No. 48. She worked at Simpson's tileworks next to the White Swan in Middleport. His father, also Harold, was a miner. Now lives at Heyburn Crescent, Dale Hall.

Date of interview: 4/6/2003.

From the age of five, I attended Middleport Infants School. In the morning, we were given milk and we played in the playground at the rear. The milk, a third of a pint, came in a small glass bottle. It used to be delivered to the Co-op warehouse at the end of Newport Lane, which was also the bakery[1]. A man used to deliver the milk around the streets of Middleport, in a handcart, and he would drop several crates off at the school.

I went to Longport Junior School from the ages of eight to eleven. You didn't have to take any schoolbooks then, and pens and pencils were provided. There was no homework, and so no need for satchels. Some of the Longport school pupils would attend without any shoes.

Every year, during the spring or summer, the headmaster of the school would address the pupils. His speech varied little from year to year, and concerned swimming in the Trent and Mersey Canal. He would say, "You must not swim in the canal water. It is 'doggy-broth'". If people didn't want their dogs, they would often throw them into the canal in bags, weighed down by bricks, whilst they were still alive. Sometimes I actually saw dead dogs floating on the water surface. I couldn't swim myself, but saw quite a few other children in the canal.

Sometimes, my parents would buy me a fishing net and I would take a jam jar and fish in the canal. Another favourite pastime was to go 'dredging' in the canal. We would use the grocer's ropes and attach a hook on the end, which was usually an old bucket handle. We would pull out any old rubbish, including bicycle frames, from the bed of the canal. On a nice day, you would probably see about half a dozen children along various places on the canal, all dredging.

As children, we were also familiar with Burgess and Leigh's shraff tip, which was unprotected by any gate. It was open. Broken ware and saggar remains used to be loaded on to a large-wheeled cart at the manufactory, and taken by horse down to the tip. The chap who did it would often throw two or three shovels of small coal on the waste tip, and locals used to scramble among the rubbish to get it out so that they could take it home for the fire. I suspect that the ostler was doing this surreptitiously for the benefit of local people. I don't suppose Burgess and Leigh would be too pleased. Sometimes, we used to make a fireplace from three bricks and a few sticks. we would use some of the coal and make a fire there on the tip.

Later, I attended Middleport Senior School, where the boys and girls were

Middleport in 1951, during the
filming of *The Card*
*Courtesy of Harold Gordon.*

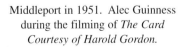

Middleport in 1951. Alec Guinness
during the filming of *The Card*
*Courtesy of Harold Gordon.*

segregated. The side of this overlooked what was then Stanley Street. The boys occupied the first floor schoolrooms, and the girls were accommodated beneath. The playing areas were also separate. I recall the music teacher, Mr Chadwick who was strict. He would take pupils to the front of the class and grasp you by the hair above your ear.

Practically every teacher had a stick, and I had it a couple of times. However, even the worst-behaved children would not dare to use cheek to the teachers. During P. E. periods in the schoolyard, you played with balls and were given a sash or band made of strong tape which you placed diagonally across your body for team games.

The canal bridge just above the McGuinness's scrap metal business was known to us as Pidduck's bridge. Walk over the present bridge towards Longport, and you will see the street sign 'Pidduck Street' on the building on your left hand side. This building was Pidduck's (later Price's) bakery. Around the corner to the left was Bridge Street, which is now Milvale Street.

When I was a small child, Peacock's stall in the Covered Market used to sell children's toys. The pressed tin toys were about a penny each, and were a treat for me. These were little toy motor cars, made of old and probably rejected tin. If you looked inside some of the cars, you could even see the printing which had originally been put on the tins. In later years, I occasionally purchased 'Dinky' cars from Tiley's in Market Place, for about sixpence.

There was once a marlhole where Heyburn Crescent is now. One day, at school, news spread that a horse had fallen into the marlhole, and was floating in it, blown up like a barrage balloon. By the time I reached the scene, a day or so later, it was dead. The driver of the horse and cart, which had belonged to a little farm down at the Sytch, had been tipping into the marl hole, and had got too close. The horse and cart had then fallen into the hole.

When I was a little older, we children would ask local grocers for the plaited rope which was used to tie up their orange boxes, and we'd hang it from gas lamp-posts. We'd then make a loop in the rope so that we could sit in it, or hook one leg in it, and use this as a swing. It was possible to clamber up the lamp-posts, by using the small ladders attached to them. Someone would push you round and round, as if it were a maypole, and then you would swing around the other way, and the rope would unwind. We did this in Navigation Street and other streets nearby. At the time, there were no swings in Middleport, even in the park.

In my early teenage years, my friends and I used to play football on the Burslem Albion pitch which was where McGuinness's is now. We'd play there till lunchtime, go home for lunch, and then continue in the afternoon. There were goalposts, but it was a well-worn area with about seventy per cent of it free of grass! Another patch of ground near Barnfields was used for football, too, and was known by us as 'the Celtic'. Higher up, on the Grange, was another pitch, but it had a severe slope.

I was a newspaper boy for Cartledge's newsagents' shop in Hitchen Street, which no longer exists. It lay between Navigation Street and Wharf Street. All paperboys were required to have a card and badge, with your own number on. The badge was perhaps about the size of an old halfpenny piece. You had to collect these from Hanley Town Hall, if you wanted to take newspapers. You were not allowed to sell any newspapers, even if someone asked for one on your round. You could only deliver.

We newsboys used to collect money for Mr Cartlidge on Sundays, sometimes as much as £2. I never heard of any newsboy having his money stolen from him. We carried a little book in which the customers' payments were ticked off. At our shop, we had different rounds for the morning and the afternoons. I occasionally had to deliver papers to the signalman's box at Longport railway station. The house-numbers were marked up for us on the morning newspapers, but we were not given any list of house-numbers for the Evening Sentinel delivery, later. You had to do the round from memory.

Our family shopped at the Co-op shop right opposite Middleport WMC in Newport Lane. There wasn't a great deal of fruit and vegetables sold there, but you could buy flour, tea, potatoes and tinned goods. They would weigh your sugar in the shop, and would cut your cheese whilst you waited. Bacon was sliced according to the thickness you required. You could do the family's weekly shop there. There was also the huge Co-op emporium in Queen Street, Burslem, which sold mainly clothing, rather than food. We also used the Meat Market behind the Old Town Hall. It used to be open until 9 pm or 10 pm on a Saturday nights in the late 1930s. In those days, there were not the freezing facilities there are now, and so people would wait around in the last hour, waiting for the meat to be sold at a cheaper price.

I remember the roof of the Palace Cinema collapsing from the weight of snow above it. Fortunately, the cinema had been closed for the day, on account of the death of King George V in 1936. The news spread like wildfire in Burslem.

I attended Sunday school until I was about fifteen, at the Middleport Memorial Methodist chapel in Newport Lane. Drink was condemned by Methodist groups in those days, and you were asked to abstain from drinking. It wasn't a binding agreement on account of my young age, but I signed the 'pledge' provisionally when I was twelve. I have kept it ever since.

I started work at what was then known as the Manchester Pottery of George Wade, in Burslem High Street (later Greenhead Street). I started as an apprentice fitter and turner from the age of fourteen. Before I was even fifteen, I was working twelve-hour nights for six nights a week, on 'war work'. During the War, the only way you could keep a fitting shop operational, was by doing 'war work'. We used to turn parts of tanks. I worked at Wade's between 1941 and 1943, before going to work in Stoke.

Notes:
1) This premises is referred to as 'Flour Mills' on the 1924 Ordnance Survey Map, and the building complex (which later accommodated the Morrilew Pottery) still stands.

Middleport in 1951, during the filming of *The Card*
*Courtesy of Harold Gordon.*

Middleport in 1951, during the filming of *The Card*
*Courtesy of Harold Gordon.*

Peter Heath and his Victorian musical box in Burslem.  (4/12/2002)

The Red Lion in Burslem, December 2003.

## 9. IDA HEMMINGS

Born Ida Machin, 11/1/1928, in Wellington Street (now Auckland Street), Burslem and later moved in the same street. Her parents were Samuel and Laura Machin. She went to schools in Burslem. She moved to Waterloo Road when she married.

Date of interview: 22/7/2003.

When I was growing up, parties were organised in Wellington Street to celebrate jubilees and coronations. Tables would be placed down the centre of the street. Children also swung on lamp-posts using orange-box rope. In our street, Mrs Dean ran a shop which sold flour, bacon, sugar, tea and other groceries. Children went there for toffee.

I recall the Hippodrome cinema at the top of Scotia Road. I would go to the Saturday afternoon matinees, and on occasions, we were given an apple and an orange. I would go again in the evening with mother if there was anything on worth watching.

W. F. Kent's factory was in our street and the firm produced items such as porcelain electrical switches. One of my very first jobs involved working in their warehouse wrapping up switches in brown paper and packing them into tubs with straw in. I was paid £4 a week when I first started, and worked there from fourteen to seventeen.

I worked at St John's C of E School as a caretaker between 1967 and 1988, when I was sixty. I attended to the coke boilers and cleaned the windows and floors. I cleaned the offices, staff room, toilets, cloak room and three classrooms. On Sunday mornings, I would go and rake all the coke out of the two boilers, and prepare them for lighting on Sunday evening. The school would then be warmed up for the following day. One boiler was underground and reached by a set of steps at the side of the school. I had to wait until it had 'caught' and then stoke it up and push the dampers in to keep it going overnight.

When I returned to my house in Waterloo Road, I would look for the smoke emerging from the chimneys. If it was, then I knew that the boilers were fine. Another job was to clear thick snow from the paths to the school entrances in the winters. The salt would be down on the paths before the children arrived. I also made sure that the gates were open for the milkman in the mornings.

The images in this chapter are of Kent's Novelty Works in Wellington Street, Burslem.
*Courtesy of Geoff Rigby.* Above: Part of the Die-fitting dept. Below: Turning and fettling shop.

Above: Mr W.F. Kent of Kent's Novelty Works. The firm of William Kent was established in 1878 and the partners were W.F. Kent, E.J. Kent & S.H. Kent. It manufactured all kinds of porcelain articles for electrical engineers, and brass and iron founders.

Placing saggars in the oven.

Glaze blowing dept.

The Sliphouse.

Figure pressing shop.

No 1 pressing shop.

No 2 pressing shop.

Fettling shop.

Placing ware in saggars.

Dipping house.

Courtesy of Robert Brookes

Gibbs' Clockmaker & Jewellers, Dale Hall,
early 20th century.

## 10. ROSEMARY KIRKBRIDE

Born Rosemary Ina Austin, 27/6/1923, in Davenport Street, Trubshaw Cross. She married Brian in 1949. They now live in the Westlands.

Date of interview: 21/11/2003.

I was born on a pottery manufactory's premises. This was Thomas Hughes and Son's Unicorn Works, in Davenport Street, Longport[1]. I still have a few pieces of pottery made by Hughes, including a chamber pot.

My father Frederick Austin was the lodge-man, and it seems, the 'trouble-shooter', as everyone seemed to come to him if anything went wrong. The work people called him 'the Sergeant', as he, along with his two brothers, had been in the 18th Hussars and taken part in the Boer War.

We lived in the lodge house attached to the works. Its entrance led into a small office with a big desk and a lovely big fire. This was my father's office, although he was not in it very often. If you went through a door, and then a passage, you came into our hall. We had what we called in those days a front room, or best room. Then there was a living room and a kitchen. Upstairs, there were four bedrooms, including my brother's at the top of the stairs. There were folding doors in between my bedroom and my mother's.

There was no bathroom in those days. There was a yard outside, and we kept chickens there. We kept about ten, and two cockerels. They used to walk about the factory. We called one of the cockerels 'the fighting cock', for he could be aggressive if he wanted to be. One day, when mother was hanging washing out, he pecked a piece out of her leg - so we had him for Christmas dinner, later that year.

On Friday night, the wages would be sent down to my father's office, and I used to help him to spread them out on the desk. The workers at the factory would have to come in through a little gate if they wished to clock off and on in the office. Some hung their clothes up in the coat-room. The lodge house had glass windows. In front of the lodge, there was a weighing machine for the horses and carts. They would be weighed on this before they went out to pick up coal or other goods, and would then be weighed again when they returned with their burden. Nearby, crates would be stacked up, for packing ware in. They were made on site.

At around five o'clock in the evenings, a friend and I used to play on the works. We would often get lost, as there were corridors and rooms all over. There was no actual security presence, although of course, the bottle ovens had to be fired throughout the night, and Mr. Parr attended to this. He was a tall man, with a pipe. Sometimes, he would stroll down to our lodge for a chat - as did the police constable from Burslem. The factory was on his beat, and he would warm himself by our coal fire.

I went to St. Paul's School, Elgreave Street, Dale Hall. Mr. Jennings was the headmaster.

Every Christmas, my father, who rarely went shopping, took the rest of us to James Norris's wine and spirit merchants in Market Place, Burslem[2]. We would buy our

Christmas drinks from there. On the counter were piles of blue willow pattern plates. For every bottle of port or sherry you purchased, you were given one of these plates. I still have five, all dated 1930.

Saturday afternoon was a great day for local children. We used to go to the Palace Cinema in Burslem, where for 2d. we could see the matinee. When it finished, all the lights came on, and we were all turfed out in readiness for the evening performance. The attendants would go round with a big spray, and disinfect the place. Some of the young boys would hide under the seats, as they wished to stay in for the next performance. The attendants were wise to this and would tip the seats up and chase them out.

On Saturday night, our parents used to take us to Burslem Covered Market, and we would buy all our fruit and vegetables for the coming week. During the War, we would go to Woolworths for the weekly sweet ration.

On Sunday mornings in the 1930s, my father would get dressed in his Sunday best, and one of the lorry drivers at the factory would take him out in his car to local pubs. Dad didn't drink very much, but it was a social affair. They would call at the Staff of Life in Dale Hall[3], followed by the Leopard and the New Inn in Burslem. The owner of the New Inn was my godfather, Mr George Spedding, a dapper little man who always wore spats. I would often be taken into the back parlour and given a lemonade. Before we left, Mr Spedding would give me half a crown, which was a fortune in those days.

Notes:

1) Hughes, Thomas and Son, Unicorn Works, Davenport Street, Longport, in the 1912 directory.

2) James Norris (Burslem) Ltd, Wine and Spirit Merchants, Ale and Porter Bottlers, were established in 1879. (The Burslem Traders' Association Souvenir Programme to commemorate the Coronation of Queen Elizabeth II, 1953).

(3) The Staff of Life was demolished in 1996.

St Paul's Church, Dale Hall, Burslem.

Courtesy of May Frost

Mrs Bott, probably in the 1950s, with
St Paul's Church in the background.

St Paul's National School, in Ellgreave Street, Dale Hall, c. 1928. *Courtesy of Rosemary Kirkbride.*

## 11. SYD LAWTON

Born 30/3/1946 at Cornhill, Ball Green. His father, George Lawton was a fireman at Chatterley Whitfield Colliery and was later a commissionaire at the Coliseum cinema in Burslem. Mother, Alice (nee Hargreaves), worked in the pottery industry. As a child, Syd lived in Stonor Street on the Grange Estate, Cobridge, and afterwards other addresses including 21 May Street, Burslem (off Hamil road and above Vale Park) where he lived for three spells. He also lived at Stoke and Trent Vale. He kept the Swan in Burslem from 1990 until 1996, subsequently managing a snooker hall in Merrial Street, Newcastle. He ran Rist's Sports & Social Club for about three years, then did factory work before coming back to Burslem to help out at the Huntsman. He managed the adjacent Ye Olde Crown for a year before he returned to the Swan in March 2001 to be his own boss.

Date of interview: 12/10/2003.

I attended three schools, beginning with St. Peter's Infants in Cobridge. I then moved to North Road Juniors in Cobridge, and finally, Moorland Road Secondary Modern from the age of eleven to fifteen.

The very first school excursion I remember saw the pupils of North Road School leaving the old Cobridge Railway Station and spending a day in Rhyl. We took packed lunches. The train journey, alone, was a great experience for the children.

Along with other children, I trespassed in the crate yard on the Grange. There were logs which were allowed to soak in about two feet of water, prior to being cut up. There were perhaps a couple of dozen, and they seemed massive to children of our age. We used to jump from log to log, and if we fell in, we wouldn't go home for two hours, until we had dried out. There were the 'V-banks' on the Grange. The name referred to the fact that there were two hills, which formed a 'V'. We would play cowboys and indians or soldiers there for hours.

When our family lived on the Grange estate, I was often sent by my father to Seddon's which was just below the Stag public house and is now a small bakery. Seddon's was a mens' and boys' outfitter's. We would perhaps buy a duffel coat or a pair of trousers - whatever we might be short of.

Nearby on Waterloo Road was Noel Tracey's grocery shop[1]. I saw cash-carriers for the very first time in this shop. Mr Tracy would often have a pencil behind his ear, and he would rattle off your purchases - cheese, butter, bacon - like an auctioneer. He would put your money into the cash-carrier, pull a cord, it would go up to the desk upstairs, and you would receive your change in return with a little note which you would take home to your parents. Actually, he could reckon money up quicker than the cashiers upstairs.

I was also sent on errands to Caney Mayer's general grocer's shop at the end of Stonor Street, taking the Wartime ration book. I discovered later that Caney gave our family items for which he received no payment at the time. A couple of days later, I would take the money up to him. I didn't realise what it was to be having items 'on tick'. He probably didn't do this for everyone on the estate, as it wouldn't have been feasible.

I loved Moorland Road School. I recall Nobby Baxter, the assistant headmaster and Walter Chadwick, who we used to call 'Mad Chad'. He taught religious instruction and music and was always very strict but very fair. He was only a short fellow, and most of the thirteen and fourteen year old lads were almost as tall as him. However, it didn't matter whether some of the boys were bigger than him or not - he ruled his classroom. He missed nothing. If the slightest thing was out of place, he would be down on you like a ton of bricks. Sometimes, he rapped me across my knuckles with his ruler for being inattentive. If he was speaking about music, he liked your undivided attention.

Another teacher I held in great esteem was Alf Jenkins, the finest teacher who taught me. He taught history and was also a sports master who loved cricket. He was a gentleman, a gentle giant, standing well over six feet tall, probably weighing about twenty stone - physically imposing, but very warm. He would do anything to enable his pupils to enhance their abilities. He set me on the right road, the straight and narrow.

School equipment at Moorland Road was very basic. There were pens and inkwells, and desks with lift-up lids. The books would be kept inside. For sport, we would use the assembly hall. Sometimes, football and cricket would be played on Sneyd Hill, where there were pitches for both. I suspect that Sneyd Cricket Club rented it out to the school when the pitch was not being used. There was a proper pavilion, and so we used to feel as if we were playing at Lord's.

I was about six or seven years old when I attended my first Port Vale match. From leaving home in Stonor Street, on the way to Hamil Road, there was a sea of black and white scarves and rosettes. I found the atmosphere magical. Whatever had happened at the match would keep me talking all weekend, and I must have driven my parents mad. Roy Sproson was my favourite player without doubt. I always call him Sir Roy Sproson. I had knighted him. He was a wonderful player at left-half or left-back, a great club man[2].

At the age of about thirteen I became a ball-boy at Vale Park. I remained so for twelve or eighteen months. There was a winger called Brian Jackson, who asked me to take a brand new pair of football boots home, to break them in for him. He said: *"Here you are, son. Take the boots home with you, and ask your parents if you can walk around in them - upstairs, in the lounge, anywhere. Then bring them back to me in three weeks' time"*. He wanted his boots softened up. I wore them over the top of my shoes for about three weeks; I would walk up and down the stairs in them. Mother had passed away by then, but Dad was a Vale fanatic and was probably as chuffed as I was. I felt ten feet tall for three weeks. I took them back and received a pat on the head.

On match-days, my job would be to collect the ball if it went out of play and return it as fast as I could. We wore track-suits, which may have been cast-offs from old players. Mine was about two or three sizes too big, and they got very heavy if it was raining. We wore Vale shirts beneath, but we had to provide our own boots. Afterwards, we brushed the dressing rooms out, and gathered up the players' kits. We would take the soiled strips to a boiler room and place them in sacks for a kit lady to collect them and take home to wash. We ball-boys would also clean the boots and hang them back on the dressing-room pegs. Len Parton, the groundsman, was our boss. He lived on the Park estate and was very regimental in his ways. He wore a long, gabardine coat and a trilby and was a wonderful groundsman - so much so, that he was eventually poached by Stoke City when Tony Waddington was the manager.

I had my very first drink of beer at the Roebuck pub when I was fifteen years old. Perhaps I looked older than my age, or just a sensible lad, but they served me in there. I had left school and was working at Howell's electric motors at Vale Place, Cobridge. After a few weeks there, the older chaps persuaded me to go with them to the pub. I recall being in the Roebuck, and trying to keep below eye-level from the window - my father was working at Wade's pottery in Burslem at the time, and I didn't want him to see me when he had left the factory at 5.30 pm, walking back home. He wouldn't have approved of my drinking, and would have skinned me alive had he known!

When I started earning a little more money, I used to be able to afford to go to the Port Vale away games. My friends and I would meet in the Roebuck, and make arrangements in there, before going to the railway stations at Burslem or Longport.

Burslem was buzzing in the 1960s. There was the Adulte Club and the Embassy (which later became the 007). There were many groups playing music in Burslem at this time. I played in one myself, as drummer with Carl Mann and the Candymen. My brother, Frank Lawton, was the vocalist, singing as Carl Mann. We were the very first group to play at the Golden Torch ballroom in Hose Street, Tunstall in 1965, when we supported Billy J. Kramer and the Dakotas. We used to love playing songs by Little Richard, Chuck Berry, Gene Vincent, Fats Domino and Eddie Cochrane. We played in tight drainpipe trousers, and shirts as loud as we could find.

Our band played the Embassy and the Queen's Hall in Burslem on many occasions on Saturday nights, and a few times at the Adulte. At the Queen's, the acoustics were very good, and our sound was impressive. I had a Premier drum-kit. There was always a grand piano on the stage at the Queen's, and so on these occasions, our keyboardist would leave his organ in our van, and play the piano instead. We loved it, because we felt we sounded better with the piano accompaniment.

Patrons paid admission on the door, and there would perhaps be about 2,000 people in the Queen's Hall on Saturday nights. The bands of Ken Jones and Reg Bassett would often appear with support from a group such as ours. Up until the 1960s, the big bands were all the rage, but afterwards, groups became very popular. There might be four different groups on at the Queen's on a Saturday night in the late Sixties. Eventually, the groups took over, which made some people very sad, but the teenagers of the day wanted to drink and dance in these auditoria.

The Queen's was quite vast. There was a big dance floor area with tables and chairs around it. There was a balcony above, with the bar being upstairs. You fetched your beer and then came back down to the dance floor. On occasions, there might be a scuffle between teddy boys arguing over a girl, but situations such as these were well-controlled.

Notes:
1) Tracey, Thos. Saml., grocer, 80, Waterloo Road, is listed in Kelly's (1940).
2) Bycars Park was officially renamed Sproson Park, April 2002, as a tribute to the Sproson family.

The Millstone Inn in the Market Place, which became Lloyd's Tavern.

Below: The New Inn, Market Place, Burslem. Early 20th century.

The Swan Hotel, Swan Square, in the process of demolition before rebuilding.
*Courtesy of David Riley.*

The bar inside the Swan Hotel, before its rebuilding. *Courtesy of David Riley.*

The Swan Hotel, Swan Square, before rebuilding. *Courtesy of David Riley.*

Outside the Swan Hotel before it was rebuilt.
*Courtesy of David Riley.*

St John's Church, Burslem.

## 12. BETTY MACHIN

Born Margaret Betty Paton, 11/1/1928, in Darlaston on the A34 between Stone and Newcastle. Has always preferred to be known as Betty. Her father, a Scotsman, was William Reid Paton. Her mother, Ethel May Davies, was from Cobridge. She had two younger sisters, Dorothy and Jean. She taught Physical Education at Moorland Road School in Burslem for 17 years.

Date of interview: 25/6/2003.

When I was four, our family went to live in Sneyd Street, which ran from Sneyd Green down to Cobridge. We lived in a house directly opposite Sneyd Green Schools. One of my earliest memories is sliding down the dirt of Sneyd Colliery's waste tip. Mother didn't mind too much, as she was very happy-go-lucky. I played mostly in the garden as a child, but I had a pedal car on the pavement in our road. It was something of a status symbol, and I was very popular with the boys!

My first school was Sneyd Green Infants, and afterwards, the Junior section. They were in two blocks in the same yard. I only had the cane once. Someone in our class had committed an indiscretion, and nobody would own up to it, and so most of the pupils were caned. I hadn't done anything wrong, but nevertheless, I received little sympathy when I returned home.

I received a good standard of education at the school, as I knew English, I could knit and sew, and I knew all my multiplication tables up to 'twelve times'. The maths teacher, Mr Sergeant, had a graph on a back wall in the classroom, which included the pupils' names in alphabetical order. A pupil who had progressed to his or her 'four times' table, for instance, was awarded four stars on the graph. It was a race to see who could reach twelve stars first.

When I was eleven, we moved to Albany Road West, now known as Northam Road, which was on the fringe of Birches Head.

Eighteen of us from Sneyd school passed our scholarships, and so at the age of eleven, the girls entered Brownhills High School for Girls, and the boys went to Hanley High School.

Just before the war broke out, and in my last year at the Sneyd Green schools, trestle tables were erected in the main hall and they put various parts of gas masks on them, ready to be assembled. I remember making them up. Before I attended the school at Brownhills, I recall going to school carrying my satchel and my gas mask, which was contained within a cardboard box. I started at Brownhills in 1939 when the war began, and leaving at the age of sixteen.

I found time to become involved with the Womens' League of Health and Beauty, and I was a member for over twenty years. We met at the Queen's Hall, Burslem, and also organised shows there. The organisation also ran a Mothers and Daughters class, and photographs were taken of us.

Though I was unqualified as a teacher, I was offered the chance of teaching physical education at the Orme Girls School in Newcastle in 1962, afterwards teaching the same subject at Queensbury School, Longton. I taught there until the school closed in 1963, before moving to Moorland Road Junior High School in Burslem, whose headmistress was Mrs Pollard. Shortly after, it became known as Moorland High School. I taught P.E. there right up until 1980.

Out in the school yard, there was a netball court. Sadly, it was used as a staff car park for most of the time. I also taught dancing in the assembly hall - Old English country dancing, and barn dancing. I sometimes taught tennis in Burslem Park, too. I normally wore a track suit whilst teaching, but at exam times, I would wear a skirt for a change.

We regularly took a bus down to the Trubshaw Cross playing fields, sometimes as often as four times a day, and my classes took place there. I trained in 'keep-fit' at Burslem Drill Hall in Newcastle Street.

In the 1970s, a new sports hall was built for us behind the junior school in Lingard Street. There was a full netball and volleyball court, and pupils were ordered to wear plimsolls on account of the special floor surfacing. I taught the girls mainly, although I refereed many a boys' inter-form football match. Eric Abberley, cousin of the Sentinel's John, was the P.E. teacher for the boys.

I always said that I would never treat a girl any worse than I would treat my own daughter. I was fair. Only once did I ever strike a girl, as she addressed me with very bad language in class. I slapped her across the face, and told the deputy headmistress, Miss Boden, that I had done it. She was shocked, but I said I wouldn't stand for that sort of thing. Later on, we found the girl, and she apologised. We were friends after that. I retired from teaching P.E. in 1980. At the age of 52, I had had enough!

## 13. TONY MOSS

Born 24/11/1945, the daughter of Edward and Elizabeth Moss, at the Dolphin public house, High Street (now Greenhead Street), Burslem. His father ran Wolstanton WMC for a while. The family moved to Smallthorne whilst he was still an infant, and he was educated at Smallthorne Infants school, Chell Heath Junior school and then Park Road senior school in Burslem. He has kept the White Swan pub in Middleport since 1989.

Date of interview: 17/6/2003.

The pub in which I was born was one of two Dolphins in central Burslem. It used to stand directly opposite an abattoir, and the covered entry which leads to the Old Town Hall. The family left the Dolphin shortly after I was born. As a child, I remember it still standing, but boarded up. It was later demolished and Wade's manufactory built a car park there[1].

During my childhood, I spent a lot of time in Burslem, as my grandfather lived in Scotia Road. Mother used to buy lead toy soldiers or marbles for me, from Woolworth's in Burslem.

I spent a lot of time playing in that area during the school holidays. We used to go up to Wade's tip, and pick out the little Whimsey figures. They were seconds, of course, but it was fun for us to collect them[2]. We often wandered afterward to Bradwell Wood with a pack of sandwiches and spend the day there. We would walk up Chatterley Street to the allotments situated just off Westport Road. A few pigs were kept there, and we used to feed them with potatoes.

I often went on the Scotia WMC club trips in the 1950s. The trains left from the Loop line station in Moorland Road, passed through Hanley and then joined the main line at Etruria and proceeded to Blackpool. You would be given a bottle of pop and a bag of crisps to take on your journey there, and half-a-crown in spending money, which was quite a lot of money!

I attended Park Road secondary school between the ages of 11 and 15. They were wonderful days. The boys and girls were segregated in the school playground by a great gate with a bolt on. We used to go up to the nearby school in Jackfield Street for school dinners, as our school did not have cooking and dining facilities at the time. We shared the other school's dining room. The teachers sat in the middle, with the pupils and other tables all around them.

I used to smoke, and during our dinner hour, I'd sometimes call at a little shop directly opposite Park Road school, where they sold what were known as 'joysticks'. These were cigarettes about nine inches long, which we would cut up into three lengths for three of us. We would then smoke these in Burslem Park. I was never caught smoking at school, though. Other pupils brought sachets of orange cordial from the shop, to mix with the water they were given during the lunch hour.

I remember the art teacher, Alfie Lake, and Miss Woollam, who taught religious instruction. Mr Alcock taught P.E., and Mr Simonds taught music. I went to visit Mr

Leopard Hotel, Market Place, Burslem, owned by the brewers Allsopp & Sons. c. 1903.

The Bull's Head in St John's Square (2/5/2001). It is owned by the Burslem based brewery, Titanic.

The American pub in Waterloo Road, Burslem, August 1989. It was renovated and reopened as the American Clubhouse, a centre for people with mental health needs in 2000.

Simonds at his house in Cellarhead during the school holidays. I spent my last year at school primarily in Mr Grant's joinery class. He would pick two pupils who were good at the subject and who might work in that field when they left school. I helped Mr Grant in the woodwork class, and did little jobs for the school. I also did maths and P.E. I left school and for a short time, I was an apprentice joiner at Wood and Sons in Burslem.

The P.E. lessons were held in the assembly hall, where there were ropes and medicine balls. We played football at Trubshaw Cross playing fields, and I played for the school football team as a goalkeeper. Sometimes the matches against other schools were played in school time, but on other occasions, they were played after school, and superintended by the teachers.

We were also taken to Burslem swimming baths in Moorland Road. We earned certificates for retrieving a brick from the bottom of the pool and swimming several lengths. The girls went to the baths with the boys. There were ground floor changing cubicles. The boys were on one side, and the girls on the other. There was a balcony for spectators, and on some occasions after school, I would watch the water polo matches with my friends.

I was only punished with the cane once. A friend and I were larking about in the toilets, and I was stopping him exiting, by holding the door handle. Mr Hall gave me two lashes on the palm of the hand. Funnily enough, I was a school prefect at the time! There was a head boy, a head girl, and a small number of prefects who were chosen in their last year at school.

I began courting Jennifer when I was sixteen, and I married her when I was 22. We would often visit the Leopard for a couple of drinks before going to the Queen's. During our courtship, we would go on alternate Saturdays to the Queen's in Burslem and the King's Hall in Stoke. Among the bands I saw at the Queen's were Vince Everett and the Black Orchids. We danced on the ground floor, and bought drinks from the bar upstairs. There were seats up there, and couples often sat down and 'canoodled" I also remember Strikes, a nightclub, which used to stand in Westport Road, opposite the Huntsman. An interesting feature was the single-decker vintage bus, which was upstairs. People would be allowed to sit in the bus if they wished to. If you wanted to take a break from dancing, there was a drinking area near to the bus. We also went to the Adulte in Waterloo Road.

I enjoyed going to Vale Park, although there was no seating in those days. We stood and watched. There were tea stalls, which were just small huts, at Hamil Road End and at the Bycars End, which I favoured. I used to buy tea, bovril, crisps, or occasionally a pie. You would often see Vale players like Albert Leek and Colin Askey walking around Burslem.

Notes:
1) Kelly's (1940) lists the Dolphin Inn (Jas. Gibson), 55, High Street (now Greenhead Street) and the Dolphin Inn (Mrs. Lizzie Steele), 4, Church Street.
2) Compare this account with those of Robert Adams and Wenda Dyer.

## 14. JOY PURCELL

Born as Joy Eaves, 1938 in Westwood Road, Wolstanton. She grew up in Wolstanton and Waterloo Road, Cobridge, where she met her husband, Brian. After their marriage in 1959, they went to live in the Wolstanton house in which Joy was born. They now live in Trentham.

Date of interview: 20/1/2003.

I was born in Westwood Road, Wolstanton. My father, Joseph Eaves, had been a placer in the pottery industry, and my mother, Mary Eaves (née Mitchell) made kiln furniture. She had been a stilt-maker at Arrowsmith's factory in Burslem[1]. The Mitchells were a huge family well-known around Burslem and beyond. My maternal grandfather, James, was thought to have had about 24 children, although not all of them survived.

My first memories are of the end of the War, and being told at Granville Infants School, in Waterloo Road, Cobridge, that if we didn't learn to sing Land of Hope and Glory properly, we wouldn't be allowed to sing it when peace was declared. When victory in Europe was achieved, mother and I went to see a bonfire which had been lit just outside the Granville public house.

My parents had moved from Wolstanton to Cobridge in May 1939, to a shop in Waterloo Road. They lived at the shop until the 1960s, and everyone knew it as Eaves's[2]. They sold newspapers, sweets, cigarettes, a lot of milk, a small amount of grocery and Burgess's cakes. These were delivered from the Newcastle bakery, and at Christmas time, our living room and every other space available was full of cakes and pies. The local factories such as Myatt's and the Globe manufactory would regularly send out for them at lunchtimes.

Near to us were a chemist's, opposite, an oatcake shop which opened only at the weekend, Annie Leyland's greengrocers, Morris' grocers and more. Our main shopping was done at Hanley, though, at stores such as Lewis's, British Home Stores and Marks and Spencer's. We bought bacon and cheese locally in Waterloo Road.

As children, you could play in Portland Street for an hour and see no traffic, but Waterloo Road was always busy. We generally played on the 'Hollies', which was part of the land now occupied by Forest Park. Around Hanley Deep Pit, there were marlholes, brick kilns and allotments, but nobody bothered us. We lived next door to the railway line which connected Hanley Deep Pit with Shelton Bar, and the steam trains used to trail down, with coal wagons behind them, bringing the traffic on Waterloo Road to a halt at Granville crossings.

Especially during the War Years, there were about as many horses and carts as there were lorries going up and down Waterloo Road. Coal, bread and milk were all delivered by horse-carts, until lorries or vans increased, and straw would often fall off the lorries and on to the pavements. The drays of Parker's Brewery were also seen regularly, and some potbanks still used horse-drawn vehicles.

Courtesy of Robert Brookes

Cobridge, to the rear of the Queen's Hotel facing the bowling green. Cobridge St. Peter's FC with Father Morgan centre. Robert Brookes (now living in Wolstanton) is the goalkeeper behind the priest. Taken in 1933.

I left Granville Infants when I was eight, and it has now been demolished. I then spent two years at Cobridge Church School, and after passing the eleven-plus a year early, I went to Brownhills High School. I left Brownhills at 18, and went to teacher training college at Alsager.

I met my future husband, Brian, who was Cobridge-born, at Brown's dance studio on Waterloo Road, on the way to Burslem. I was celebrating the end of my A level exams, and went with a friend, Maureen Davies, who was in Brian's class at school. We knew each other through third parties. We began to go out with each other, and did our courting long-distance, Brian going to Birmingham University, and me doing teacher training.

Our local courting was done at the Queen's theatre in Burslem, or at Trentham Gardens, when the big bands were on. Rock and roll was just coming in, and people who danced to it were regarded as a bit of a nuisance, because they took up a lot of room! We stuck to quick-steps and foxtrots. There was Reg Bassett's band, and Harry Bruce's - quite a few of them.

We went to the pictures in Hanley, or the Palace and the Coliseum in Burslem. We also went to the Church of Christ in Macclesfield Street, Burslem, where my father was an elder. This was the highest position in the church, as there was no paid minister in the early days.

We married there on August 13, 1959. I had experienced adult baptism there, at the age of 12. I have now been a member for over fifty years, and was one of the first women officers of the church.

Notes:
1) Arrowsmith T. and Sons Ltd, stilt and spur manufacturers, 158, Moorland Road and Reginald Street, Burslem, is listed in Kelly's (1940)
2) Eaves, Mary (Mrs), newsagent, 426, Waterloo Road, Cobridge, is listed in Kelly's (1940).

Waterloo Road, Burslem, early 20th century.

'Bew's Corner' in Burslem. *Courtesy of David Riley.*

## 15. GEOFFREY RIGBY

Born 29/11/1944, and lived in Wellington Street (now Auckland Street) in Burslem until he was three; Moreton Street in Middleport; Fegg Hayes Road in Fegg Hayes; and now Stoneleigh Road in Chell. As a child he attended Middleport Methodist Sunday School in Newport Lane. He married in 1968.

Date on interview: 8/7/2003.

My first school was Sneyd Church of England School in Nile Street which I attended from the age of three-and-a-half to eleven years old. I recall that collecting various plants for our 'nature table' from the area around Sneyd Colliery. At the time, Mr Charles was the headmaster, and later, Mr Cartlidge.

One chap used to drive to the school in a van and stand outside our school gates, collecting rags and jamjars. He carried a suitcase with him, and you could have a goldfish, a colouring book or a pencil in return. My grandmother Laura Machin used to make custard and trifles for the school's Christmas parties, as she lived nearby in Wellington Street. There was a corner shop near the school run by a Mrs Wright who sold groceries and sweets.

We had very little equipment. We had two playing yards, one for the boys and one for the girls but no sporting facilities. The cricket and football were played on the red ash at Cobridge Park which we had to walk to. The school hall was used as a classroom and a nursery, but there was no equipment aside from a climbing frame for the young ones and a few mats for P. E. lessons.

When I visited my grandmother's house, I often undertook three particular jobs. In those days, you didn't buy salt in containers, and so my task was to grate a block of salt into stoneware jars. I also helped her to use her mangle during the washing of clothing, and my final job was to cut up squares of newspaper for behind the toilet door. I then had to put a hole in them with a skewer attach a piece of string to them and hang them on a nail on the toilet door. My grandmother's toilet was a shed-type structure at the bottom of the yard, and was covered. Also in this shed was a boiler which she lit fires underneath to produce her hot water for washing. She then had to take the hot water out of it in buckets to pour into the dolly tubs.

One man called at peoples' doors selling shoe-laces and boot-polish, and another toured the streets on his bicycle, sharpening knives and scissors.

In Nile Street, there were stables kept by Parker's brewery. They were kept by Mr Sutton, who drove a pony and trap. We children often played in the hay-lofts. Nearby, there was a pub on the corner of Waterloo Road and Pitt Street called the Bull's Head, and I recall it being kept by Mrs Littlehales. My aunt used to finish work, and clean Kent's offices in Wellington Street[1] in the evening, and have four or five pints at the pub before she went home.

My next school was St. John's Church of England School which was demolished a few years ago, and replaced by a single story building belonging to Heath's. The infants'

Sneyd C of E Junior School 1953/54.  *Courtesy of Geoff Rigby.*

school still survives adjacent the church. I attended the school until I was fifteen. We had no sports facilities, and football and cricket were played at the Grange where there were goalposts but no nets. Afterwards, we were perhaps one of the first schools to use Trubshaw Cross playing fields. It was the first time we pupils had ever seen showers during school hours! We also walked up to the baths in Moorland Road. Again, the sexes were separated in the schoolyard.

I recall Mr Forrester, the headmaster, and Mr Taverner [sic] who took pupils (about thirty at a time) on camping trips to Anglesey. This was intended as a break or a holiday for the children, and he went every year.

The children also tended an allotment on the Grange. I was a prefect at the school, and one of my responsibilities was to take money up to the Co-op bank at the top of Newcastle Street.

When I was growing up in Middleport, we played in the streets or by the Trent and Mersey Canal, where there was a football field where McGuinness's scrap merchants is now. It was bare, unseeded ground. There were no playgrounds as such. I fished in the canal, and saw other people swimming in it. I also used to help the man who came to collect the contents of the wartime pig-bins in Middleport. At the top of every entry in the rows of terraced housing, there was an indent in the wall. Underneath, would be three or four of the pig-bins, and you would put all your peelings in there. Once a week, a man would come around with his cart in order to collect them and boil them up for his pigs. I helped him, although it was a smelly job.

Notes:
1) The firm of W. F. Kent was established in 1878. Based in Wellington Street, it manufactured all kinds of china and porcelain articles for electrical engineers, brass and iron founders.

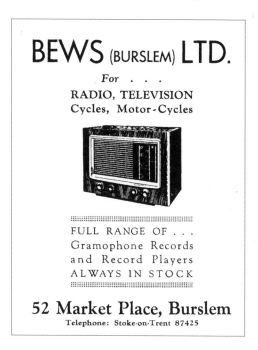

Courtesy of Robert Brookes

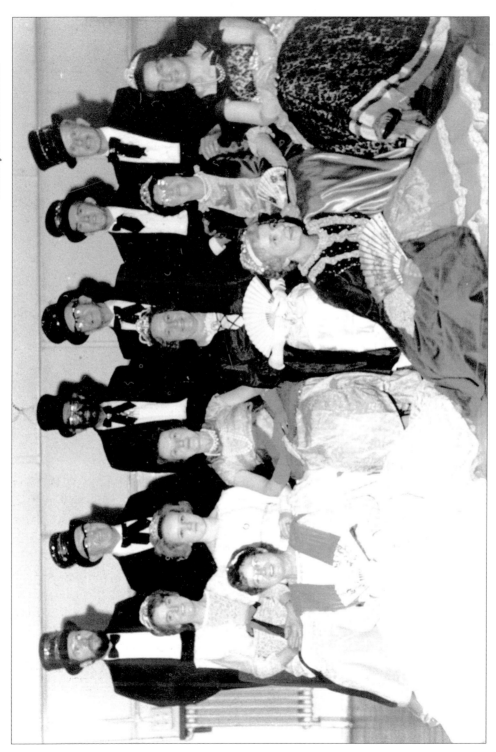

Cobridge St. Peter's concert party - probably taken at the Little Sisters of the Poor (St Augustine's). The group performed all over the Potteries. Robert Brookes is seen 'blacked up' on the back row.

## 16. IAN ROWE

Ian's father, Arthur, was born at the long-disappeared Eagle and Snake in Waterloo Road, and became a mat-maker on the Park Estate. Ian himself was born 8/1/1932 at 72, Dartmouth Street, Burslem. He moved to Wolstanton in 1953 when he married. His wife, Betty Knight, had been born in Bank Hall Road. Ian died in July, 2003.

Date of interview: 2/4/2003.

I attended Park Road School, just off Hamil Road, staying until I was 14. There were some good teachers, but I was most influenced by the art teacher, Alfie Lake. A lot of teachers used canes for punishment, but Alfie's approach didn't necessitate any punishment. He gained a lot of respect. Mind you, I was caned by other teachers for all sorts of things.

Mother used Askey's fish and game shop in Market Place, Burslem. We ate a lot of fish in those days, probably because it was cheaper than red meat. We used to do a lot of shopping in Dartmouth Street. Going from the fruit shop at the top to the Park Inn at the bottom, there were about 19 little shops, including Boyce Adams, which was equivalent in those days to a modern supermarket. Mother could do her weekly shop there. Near to where I lived in Dartmouth Street, there was a cobbler, a barber, a butcher and more. There were also lots of shops in Macclesfield Street and along High Lane. We also did a lot of shopping in Hanley, because you could catch a bus from High Lane straight in. It was just as easy as going into Burslem, and made a change.

As children, we played in Dartmouth Street, there being few cars around, and also in the area where Vale Park was built in 1950. The land there was rough, not even grassed. You could barely call it a pitch, but it did have goal posts. The surface was made up of cinders and pottery shraff, and you'd always go home with cuts and grazes.

Lower down Hamil Road, where the fire station is now, was a ground used by Burslem Albion football club, and some of my friends played for them. This was a small ground, and to reach the pitch, you entered through a door in the boarding. I know some players who progressed from the Park Road football team, to Burslem Albion, and then to Stoke City. One in particular was George Bourne, who I played football with at Park Road.

A friend of mine, Harold 'Agger' Lewis, took me to my first Port Vale match at the Old Recreation Ground behind St John's church, Hanley. We walked through the red ash by Sneyd Colliery to the ground. However, my interest in Port Vale started in earnest when they moved to Burslem. For refreshments, I used to take a flask of tea.

I made a friend of a Vale player called Tommy Cheadle, a centre-half. As a boy of about 18, I used to visit the Park Inn, and Tommy would come in, buy a drink for all of us, and have a half-pint for himself. This went on for quite a while, until he came in one evening, and said, *"This is my last night. I've been reported to the club for coming out of the Park Inn, drunk"*. Actually, I had never seen him drunk, but that was the allegation. I never saw him again, until he, as a postman, delivered the mail in Wolstanton.

Courtesy of Eric Sherratt

The Anderton Lock on the Trent & Mersey Canal.
Harold Hood, boatbuilder, is rear left.  Maxwell Savage, right, is having a coal
carrying narrow boat converted into a house boat.  Early 1950s.

After I'd come out of the army in the 1950s, I played darts for the Star, and came to know Arthur Berry. He could reel off the name of every pub in Burslem. The pub had a coke stove in the centre of the main room. Many of the patrons were rough but kind-hearted. On Saturday nights, every pub in Burslem was full, late on.

Vincent Riley was one of the well-known characters in the town. A friend of his, a taller man called Georgie King, used to walk around, looking up at the sky. Nobody knew why. The pair of them would be seen sitting on doorsteps all around Burslem.

I probably went to the cinemas at least three times per week. These would be the Burslem cinemas, as well as the 'Scratch' in Smallthorne. Burslem's 'monkey run' saw young people gathering in Queen Street, near to the Swan, and by the Leopard at the top, and in adjacent areas. The main idea was to pick up a girl, and this activity was often seen on Sunday nights. I remember that one night, about 1951, I had my eye on one young lady at the Waterloo Stores pub[1] in Waterloo Road. At one point, I went into the back yard of the pub to visit the toilet, and the girl followed me out. We stood talking. A chap then rushed out of the pub and threatened me. He threw a punch, I moved my head, and he struck the window overlooking the yard. The whole plate glass window just fell right through into the next room, where Mrs Bossons, the landlady, was playing the piano and singing *Beautiful Dreamer*. Nobody took any notice, and everyone carried on singing as if nothing had happened!

I worked at Burslem public baths for about four years. Lads were taken on and trained to be future superintendents. The superintendent was Bill Hodgkiss. I attended to maintenance and general cleaning. My strongest recollection of Burslem baths is of Sammy Pearson, who trained boxers in premises at the Park Road School. He was about six feet eight - he would stand on the floor of the deep end, and you would see his head popping out[2].

I started boxing with him at about 13 or 14, and was in one of his boxing teams for a while. There were no rings at the Park Road school, just four mats. One of the first things Sam used to say to new recruits was, 'Right. Hit me as hard as you can hit me'. You'd try and hit him, and he hit you first. He then told you, 'That's your first lesson'. He also used to say, 'I'm Mr Pearson. I'll tell you when you can call me Sam'. When you got to the point when you could call him by his christian name, you felt that you had accomplished something.

I was also in a cycling group called Burslem Wheelers at the age of 16 or 17. We would go out as a club on Sundays, and the route I enjoyed the most was from Burslem to Rudyard Lake. There would be about ten or twelve of us. The longest cycle journey I ever did was to Rhyl and back in a day. I then had four days off from work!

Notes:
(1) The Waterloo Stores, at 30, Waterloo Road (proprietor, T. Boon), in the 1912 directory.
(2) John Abberley, writing in his 'The Memory' column for the Sunday Sentinel (13/4/2003) recollected similarly. John also recalled Sammy's water polo playing career at Tunstall baths, and his sparring experiences with boxing world champion Primo Carnera.

Courtesy of Bernard Frain

Central Old Boys FC, Burslem. Date unknown. Printed on rear:
L-R. back row: E. Chetton (chairman), S. Hollinshead (capt.), B. Whitehouse, F. Hewitt, E. Hollinshead (hon. treas.),
G. Price, N. Lindsey, K. Baddaley, E. Wordley (trainer).
Front row: E. Leigh, C. Moore, T. Brammer, H. Eardley, T. Wordley. Members of the County Minor League, and winners of the Southwell Cup,
this team is composed of Old Boys of the Moorland Road school, Burslem ...also won the Minor County League Division II Cup.

Park Road Secondary Modern c.1952-53. The teacher in the middle is Alfie Lake.
*Courtesy of Eric Sherratt.*

Irene Hood, aged about 13, on the stage at Bethel Methodist Chapel being crowned Sunday School Queen, c.1947.
*Courtesy of Irene Sherratt (nee Hood).*

## 17. ERIC SHERRATT

Born 31/3/1932 in Milton. His family moved to Regent Road, Hanley, and later to Waterloo Road, Burslem when he was between seven and eight. Eric was educated in Burslem. He has several documents relating to the closure of Bethel Methodist chapel in the 1950s.

Date of interviews: 6/8/2003 and 10/11/2003.

Our family moved to Waterloo Road because we were a very large family. I had four brothers and five sisters, and we were looking for a large house to rent. We moved to an old house, but it had quite big bedrooms and a large cellar. However, there was no electricity in the house, and the toilet was halfway down a long back yard. At the bottom of the yard was a huge coalhouse, about the size of what would now be an average-size garage. The house is now demolished, but it stood next door but one to the American Hotel on its Cobridge side. Directly opposite was MacIntyre's factory which manufactured electrical porcelain.

We had a back kitchen with a boiler at one end. We had to light a fire under it, to have hot water for the washing. There was no bathroom, and we had to bring in a steel bath from outside the house. We would fill the bath with hot water boiled in kettles on our gas stove. The living room had a large, black, enamel range with an oven either side. As a result, a lot of the cooking was done in the living room, although some was done on the gas stove.

Our living room fire was kept alight almost all the time. We could afford to do this, as my father, John Sherratt, was a miner at Chatterley Whitfield Colliery and he used to receive concessionary coal. He used to receive a ton of coal per month, which would otherwise have cost five pounds. One of my memories of childhood is making sure that the fire was always kept alight by fetching the coal in, chopping sticks and emptying the ashes. The ashes were taken out every morning. If the fire did go out, I would sometimes have to get up at 5 or 6 am, if Dad was about to come in off a shift. A fire had to be lighted before we could prepare any food for him.

I also had to fetch gas mantles from the local shops. This was tricky, as they were very fragile and didn't last very long. However, they were the only means of light we had - and at times, we couldn't afford them. They were commonly sold in local hardware shops, as lots of people had gas lit houses.

Another job I had to do would now be regarded as very dangerous. Our radio-set worked off three batteries. One was called a grid bias battery of 0.28 volts, with little plugs along it; there was a high-tension battery, of 120 volts, which had little plugs on it; but the main item of equipment was an accumulator jar, containing sulphuric acid and distilled water. My job was to take this jar up to a shop in Burslem to have it recharged. It took 24 hours to charge - so you took one in, and brought one back. It used to be a common practice for children to walk through the streets with a battery containing sulphuric acid. It would be unthinkable today.

The death rate was quite high in the times I speak of, on account of the amount of disease. As soon as children were born, parents took out an insurance policy. They cost a penny from the Providence Insurance company, and would just cover death. I still have my penny policy. If the child passed away, at least you would have some money to bury it. Among the diseases children contracted were chicken pox, mumps, measles, whooping cough, bronchial problems and diphtheria. During the War period, people and especially children suffered from boils, ringworm and rashes. There was little food about, little hygiene, and little medication.

In every community, you had someone who helped deliver a baby, or lay out the dead. There were a lot of home remedies, too, with boils being 'cured' by brimstone and treacle. This was a mixture of black treacle and sulphur, and a few spoonfuls of this would often clean out your system. Boils would be treated with a bread poultice. Bread was soaked in very hot water, into a putty-like substance (kaolin), and it retained the heat. You then wrapped it in linen, and the heat drew the pus out of the boil or cyst.

There were certain ointments or disinfectants that you could buy, such as Dettol or Germolene, but everyone generally attended to their own medical needs. A lot of illness occurred through poor clothing. Sometimes you could not afford warm clothing, especially during the War years. Families wore hand-me-down clothes, and most houses had a last and bits of leather to repair shoes. On occasions, you would put cardboard in your shoes whilst you waited for them to be repaired. Even when your jumpers and cardigans wore out, you didn't discard them. Many floors were tiled, so old clothes were cut up into strips and used to make a rug with a Hessian backing. Patchwork quilts for the bed would also be made. Nothing would be wasted in our house.

Children around our back streets made a lot of their own playthings. The Grange in those days was a big area predominantly used as a pottery dumping ground. Moulds made out of chalk were often to be found there. You could cut a pattern in the moulds in the shape of a boat or a soldier. You would then melt some lead in a tin can and pour this into the mould in order to make toys which could then be painted. We also made kites, or little guns which would fire matchsticks. We would always make trollies out of boxes and old pram wheels, and go like the clappers down Bourne's Bank or Commercial Street. The Grange pond had a metal pipe going right across the middle of it, and it used to be a dare to run right across the middle of it, without falling in. There were newts, red penks and frogs in the pond. As a child, I never strayed beyond the Grange, the foot of Commercial Street and Bourne's Bank.

Parker's Brewery owned a number of shire horses, and as children, we would go and stroke them. You would see them dressed up in their regalia whenever there was a carnival, and they would walk along Waterloo Road. Pottery workers from McIntyre's and Kent's would come out of their workplaces covered in white clay. Waterloo Road fed a community, and you could buy anything you wanted in it. I feel that Burslem in those days was akin to present-day Hanley. Burslem's shops were not 'every day' shops; they didn't feed the Waterloo Road community, especially as many were poor in any case. If you wanted a new suit, you would go to Burton's in Burslem.

From Commercial Street to Swan Bank in Burslem, there was a broad range of shops over a third of a mile which suited the needs of most people. There were the American, Stag and Bluebell pubs, three cobblers, two doctor's establishments, two large grocery shops, two greengrocery shops, two hardware shops, four sweet shops, four chip shops, a general store, a post office, a butcher's, a chemist's, a Chinese laundry and many more outlets.

I remember the Chinese laundry well, because my father used to wear stiff white collars when he went out. The laundry would starch them. It stood almost opposite the Bethel chapel in the early 1940s, but it wasn't there for long.

From the age of twelve to fourteen, I landed a job delivering bread to people in Waterloo Road. Residents would order the bread, and I would collect it from a small confectionery shop called Erril's after I had finished school. I had a bicycle with a wicker basket on the front. Later, my employer had a hand-cart made for me, with a lid on. This had two wheels and two handles. I delivered the bread to those people up in the Cobridge area who were frankly higher in social class to those folks in my own community.

During the War, a trader called Mr Lane had a painting and decorating business in Waterloo Road. He had a very long yard, and at the bottom, he kept a bricked-off area where he kept some pigs. He persuaded people he knew to bring their waste round, peelings, etc, to feed his pigs. He had a big boiler, and he would boil up the waste and feed it to the pigs. Among others who worked with him in what was known locally as the Pig Club, was Ernie Travis, a local butcher[1]. When the pigs were slaughtered, a number of people in the Club received a few rashers of bacon. A butcher was required by law to state how many pigs he had slaughtered, and was answerable to the health authorities of the day. However, quite a few butchers sold what was known as 'slink' meat during the War. There was no real refrigeration system, and meat that was beginning to 'turn' found its way on to the market. Notwithstanding government regulations, there was a Wartime black market. The local policeman got his share of bacon!

In the 1940s, there were very few cars about, and only the people I would class as the 'super-rich' owned them. Mr Travis managed to buy a Jaguar when nobody else could even afford to look at a car. I was lucky in some respects, because our next-door-neighbours, the Podmores, owned a funeral undertaker's business in Waterloo Road, formerly known as Swindell's. This business had been using horse-drawn hearses, but I recall the transition to the big, black cars. I had the opportunity to look inside them, and even sit in them. Even our milk then was delivered by pony and trap, and the milkman would come with his churns, and ladel out gills or pints into jugs.

Goods from Burslem and Longport railway stations were delivered by horse and cart to Waterloo Road shops and factories. If I wanted to go to Hanley, and I could afford it, I would use the Loopline trains from Burslem station. There were buses about, but the seating was very basic, with no cushioning. However, after the War, the service improved, with double-deckers becoming common. There were several companies, including Brown's, PMT, and Tilstone's. The services were very regular, and even if you were in between bus stops, the drivers would still pick you up.

People regularly used buses, and often caught the same ones in the morning, which encouraged talking at bus stops. You soon got to know people, and you could trust folk in what was a closely-knit society. You told people everything, and your life story would come out! When cars became more common, and the Loopline closed, you became more of an isolated unit.

By the time I was eleven or twelve, I was very interested in scouting. I found out that the Bethel chapel in Waterloo Road had a very strong scout group, as well as a guides' and brownies' group. A condition of entry into the scouts was that you attended certain services. So I became involved at the Bethel chapel through the scouts, despite having been a member of St. John's Anglican church and having been in its Sunday school and choir. There was a room to the rear of the chapel with a stage at one end, which the scouts often used. This was the Doctor Cooke memorial room[2].

The scouts had a camping area on Biddulph Moor called Chapel's Farm. We would pull a trek cart carrying all our equipment from the chapel, through Chell, Brindley Ford, and Biddulph all the way up to Biddulph Moor, before we could make camp. Going down Chell bank, and trying to hold the cart back was problematic! The cart consisted of a large board on two strong wheels, two handles, and a couple of sides. Perhaps fifteen or twenty of us pulled it, until eventually, Mr Chapel loaned us a shed on his farm where we could store equipment.

I have strong memories of attending Moorland Road School in Burslem between the ages of eleven and fourteen. It was classed as a good school in those days, although it was very strict and equipment was restricted on account of the War. There was a great deal of blackboard teaching. One particular teacher earned notoriety as the chap who dispensed punishment with the cane. It would be a case of 'go across and see Mr. Hall'. He was a younger teacher, and I think he taught history. Music was taught by Mr Chadwick, Maths by Mr Spendilow and Science by Mr Cash.

It being Wartime, the school kept an allotment in Burslem Park, and vegetables were grown there. The lessons were strictly timed, and every time it was time to change, a bell would be rung. Eventually, I landed the job of bell-ringer, probably because I was a reliable character. I had to be at school before anyone else in the morning to ring the bell. I rang it again before I went home for lunch, and then on my return. I rang it during lesson-changes, and at 4 o'clock when school closed. It was necessary for me to sit in the classrooms where I could see the clock in the school assembly hall. All the classrooms were situated just off the hall, which was also used for P.E., although the woodwork room and the science laboratory were across the other side of the school yard. I left school at the age of 14 and was still wearing short trousers and a pullover. My weight was only four stones thirteen pounds, which said a lot about Wartime conditions.

After the War, many of the residents from the Waterloo Road area in Burslem were moved out to the new estate at Norton. Within the space of about ten years, a lot of old property was demolished, and the community in Waterloo Road collapsed as people were re-housed. Many of the old houses did not even have toilets. Some, such as the ones in Wellington Street, had old-fashioned 'ducket' toilets, where two people could sit together. The sewage collectors still came to some houses to collect the waste.

At Bethel chapel, I got to know one or two young girls, including my future wife, Irene Hood, who was in the choir. Her father, Harold Hood, was one of the trustees. There were only about 200 chapel members by about 1946, and it was losing Sunday scholars at the rate of about 25 a year. It was decided that the chapel was no longer viable and would have to be closed. Other chapels on the local circuit faced closure on account of the removal of the population to the new estates.

I married Irene at Swan Bank chapel in 1957, because the Bethel chapel had closed by this time[3]. For a while, the trustees and various worshippers whose chapels had closed met in peoples' houses. Sunday services were held in these houses, and my wife Irene played the piano during some of them. However, it was not convenient to have 25 or 30 people meeting in private houses. Subsequently, the Bethel congregation used a farmhouse at Sneyd Green, whose internal wall had been knocked through. This belonged to Noblett's farm, which was located off Mornington Road. A few of us were tradesmen, and I was an electrician, and so we managed to get the place operational. Quite a good congregation was established, and we held anniversaries in marquees on the farmer's ground. The trustees intended to set up a new chapel in Sneyd Green, using the proceeds of the sale of Bethel. However, much of the money was ultimately absorbed by the Burslem circuit and those who were fighting to set up a chapel in Sneyd Green only had about £1,000 for their cause. There was some resentment over this.

Funds were eventually raised and a new chapel built in Noblett Road on the old farmland. It was about 1958, and I am still a member. The farmhouse was knocked down.

Notes:
1) Travis, Chas., butcher, 420, Waterloo Road, Cobridge, is listed in Kelly's (1940).
2) William Cooke (1806-1884) was born at the New Inn, Burslem. He became a minister in the Methodist New Connexion. The Cooke Memorial School was built at the Bethel chapel in 1877.
3) Broadhurst Brothers (Burslem) bought the Bethel Chapel in 1957 [Evening Sentinel, 20/7/1991].

Noblett Road farmhouse which was used as a Methodist meeting place from 1956.
*Courtesy of Eric Sherratt.*

The Wesley Hall Methodist church, Sneyd Green, standing on the site of the Noblett Road Farm. Picture
in the 1960s prior to completion and opening.
*Courtesy of Eric Sherratt.*

Holdsworth's Cobblers in Waterloo Road,
Burslem, c.1920.
*Courtesy of Eric Sherratt.*

Holdsworth's Cobblers in Waterloo Road,
Burslem, c.1930.
*Courtesy of Eric Sherratt.*

Crane Street, Cobridge and Myott's Pottery.

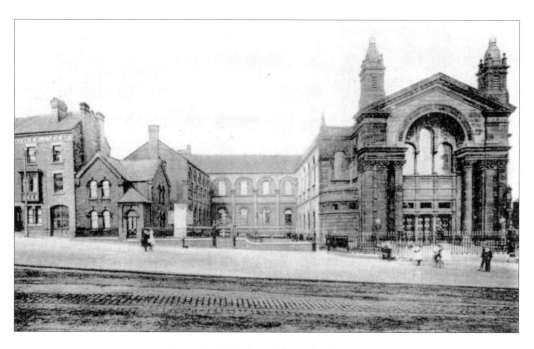

Swan Bank Wesleyan Methodist chapel.

Queen Street, 1920-1930.

Waterloo Road in the early 20th century.

A Burslem pottery
1940s.

BELOW:
Gibson's Pottery
in the 1960s.

## 18. JOAN TAYLOR

Born Joan Davenport, in Hamil Road, Burslem, 28/5/1934. She moved to Shaftesbury Avenue at the age of five, and has lived in the same house ever since. She married Brian Taylor in 1958. She spent much of her working life as a nurse and midwife.

Date of interview: 18/6/2003.

I attended Jackfield Infants school, Moorland Road junior school and finally Park Road seniors, which I left at the age of 14. Miss Coxon, a very kind lady, was the headmistress. I recall the introduction of milk bottles at playtime. Sometimes, if we were lucky, we would have a biscuit with it, but they were hard to come by as War had broken out by then. At Moorland Road juniors, we had some lessons in wooden huts, during the first year. They were separate from the main school, being in Sneyd Terrace, now Lingard Street.

I remember one teacher, Mr Liversage, being wheelchair-bound. We used pen and ink at school, and it was the monitor's job to fill the inkwells on the desks at the beginning of each week. I recall buying pen nibs from Woolworth's in Burslem, or the newsagents in Hamil Road. They were supplied by the school, but I liked writing and was a little pernickety, and so I often bought my own. I only ever had the cane once - one stroke on the palm of my hand for being late. I had been walking to school across Burslem Park, when I remembered that I hadn't taken my gas-mask with me. I knew I would be in trouble if I didn't take it, and so I went to get it, and was late for school.

At the Park Road school, Mr Bennett was the headmaster. The teachers included Mr Lake, who taught maths, Miss Woollam, who taught needlework, Mr Mountford who taught geography, and Mr Shone, the science master. Miss Owen taught needlework and other subjects including maths. Miss Cooper taught domestic science, which was lovely, we learned cooking, ironing and housekeeping skills. We made pies, cakes, and even soup.

My uncle and aunt lived next door to us in Shaftesbury Avenue. On one occasion, I asked my aunt for one of the cups my uncle Bert had won for singing. She asked me what I wanted it for. I replied that Miss Cooper had asked us to take something brass or silver, to clean. I took a silver cup to school, and when I brought it back, you could see your face in it, I had polished it so well. Uncle Bert, Herbert Mason, sang for the Burslem Orpheus Male Voice Choir. He often used to sing *Oft in The Stilly Night*. I would sit in our garden, and I could hear him singing whilst he was having a shave.

From the age of five, I was taken by my father to see Port Vale play at the 'Old Rec' in Hanley. We walked all the way from Shaftesbury Avenue. I have vivid memories of seeing the likes of Ronnie Allen and Billy McGarry playing there. I thought it was great when Vale moved to Hamil Road, much nearer our house, in 1950!

I remember going to Burslem Hippodrome, at the top of Scotia Road, when I was about five or six. Mother used to take me on Thursday nights. It was a wooden structure,

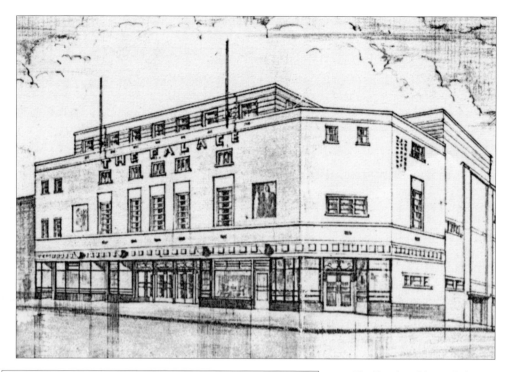

The Burslem Picture Palace. The New Palace Cinema in Cleveland Street, Burslem, opened in 1936 and was next door to the Palladium, opposite the Coliseum, and a short walk from the Moorland Picture House, Moorland Road.

The Coliseum in Burslem around 1954. It was later refurbished and renamed the Gaumont.

The two photographs on this page are from the book *Give My Regards to Broadway: More on the Picture Houses of the Potteries* by Barry Blaize, published by Churnet Valley.

and I recall seeing G.H. Eliot, 'the chocolate coloured coon', and Marie Lloyd, the singer. The auditorium had a sloping floor.

Sweets were obviously on ration during the war years, and bananas were very hard to come by. You might have some once a month if you were lucky. We lived on English apples. On Hamil Road, there was a large general store which sold a lot of fruit. It was kept by Mr Jackson, and his daughter Mary was in my class at school. When he had blood oranges in stock, they were not a rationed commodity, and so if you could get some of those, you were blown in!

Higher up Hamil Road, there was another provisions store, which is now a fruit shop. This was kept by Mr Grey. He sold 'sweet bits' and cough sweets, which were not on the ration coupons. We children used to go to Tunstall swimming baths, on Tuesday evenings, and we would buy the cough sweets and eat them on the way back.

During the war years, my mother would try to spin out a small joint of meat. She'd save just a bit for Monday, and make what our family called 'resurrection lobby'. She would take several vegetables and a tiny bit of meat, because there was a tiny bit left!

The lady who lived below our house was a big friend of my mother, and her husband was a fire-watcher in Hamil Road. So if there was an air-raid on, we'd take Nancy, the lady, and her son John into my aunt's air raid shelter next door. She felt safer with us. It was below ground, and you reached it by steps. We had put seats in it, and there were benches in case you wished to go asleep. We had an electric bulb for heating, and a gas stove, so that you could boil water and make a drink. The gas masks came in a square box attached to some twine, so that you could carry it over your shoulder. Father was in the home guard, and he kept a uniform and a gun upstairs. The room was locked, forbidden territory for the rest of us. The home guard would go through their drills on the rough land where Vale Park is now.

We children would play in Burslem Park in the evenings, but we would run in at 6.45 p.m., to listen to Dick Barton, Special Agent, on the radio. In the summertime, we would play in Finney's fields and play cricket or rounders. Girls would join in with the boys. Finney's farm was roughly where the Haywood High School is now, and there were gardens and a pool which we called 'Finney's pond' nearby. We fished in it. We would take sandwiches and stay out for quite a while, but our mothers knew where we were, and could come and shout us at any time. As long as we behaved ourselves and didn't interfere with Mr Finney's cattle, we were left alone. By the houses in what is now Cynthia Grove, there were banks of soil, dirt-banks. You could build 'houses' in between with bricks and other material.

I remember a little old lady who used to push a cart along Dolly's Lane. She would go from house to house, selling milk from the churns on her cart, in the 1940s. We purchased a lot of our fruit and vegetables from a Mr Pankhurst who lived in Broadhurst Road. He would bring his produce round in a horse and cart.

Mother would take me to the Coliseum in Bourne's Bank, Burslem when I was a little older. There were talent contests held there on Friday nights, and singers or comedians would appear. I remember the Wurlitzer organ there.

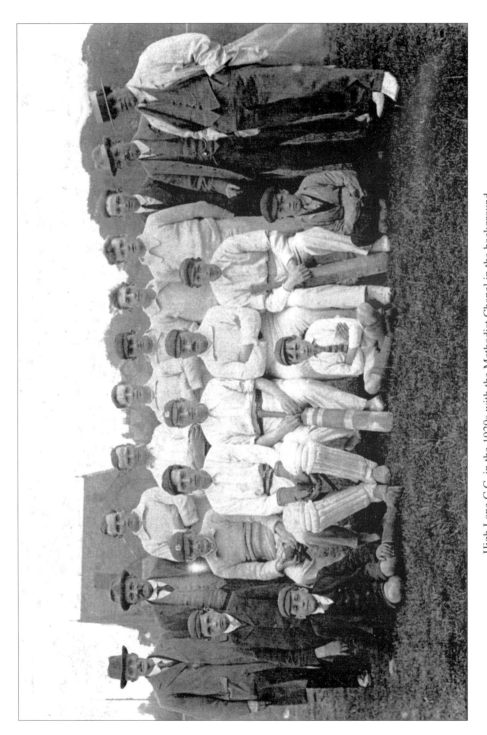

High Lane C.C. in the 1920s with the Methodist Chapel in the background.
William Boardman Senr. is on the back row, 5th from the left. William Boardman Junr. is sitting on the grass in the centre.
*Courtesy of J.M. Morris.*

Among the shops our family used in Burslem was Boyce Adams, in Market Place. This was a lovely shop, which sold bacon, cheese, butter and sugar, and they ground their own coffee. The Co-op cake shop stood where the travel agency is now, in Market Place. You went upstairs for a cup of tea or coffee. Nobody made trifles like the Co-op did. They were the old, traditional ones. There was no jelly base, it was proper fruit.

At the age of 14, I went to work for Mr Salt, who ran a chemist's shop near the foot of Dartmouth Street. There were drawers which were labelled with their contents, which you measured out for the customers. People weighed themselves on our weighing machine which came complete with weights. You couldn't buy sweets from our shop, as they were still on ration, but you could buy liquorice root. People suffering from a cough wouldn't usually go to the doctor's. They would come and ask for a bottle of Mr Salt's 'Special'. He had formulated this when his own father had been plagued by chest problems, and people swore by it as a remedy. We also sold baby food.

When I was 19, I left the chemist's, to begin training to become a nurse. I initially went to the Haywood Hospital, which in those days was a fully-fledged nursing school. I qualified as a nurse on March 31, 1958.

# George H. Salt
M. P. S.
## DISPENSING CHEMIST

SICKROOM, NURSERY
and
TOILET REQUISITES

## 24 Dartmouth Street
**BURSLEM**          **STOKE-ON-TRENT**

Telephone 84521                    Night 84308

High Lane C.C., Burslem, 1930s. The Haywood High School was later built on the site of the Cricket Club.
*Courtesy of Robert Adams.*

## 19. GEOFF WEAVER

Born 8/8/1939 in Tunstall, and grew up in Stanfields. He was educated in Burslem, and later worked as a teacher in Milton and Longton.

Date of interview: 20/8/2003.

My grandparents lived in a row of quite substantial cottages called Stanfields Cottages on High Lane. My grandfather ran a pottery haulage business, removing shraff from potbanks by horse and cart. My grandmother's father, Mr Alcock, farmed part of the Stanfields area. Before the War, they moved to opposite the new council estate, at 139, Haywood Road, Burslem.

Entertainment meant going to the Coliseum cinema in Burslem, calling in at the Wright's pie shop afterwards, and home again. However, my main entertainment as a child involved running wild over the fields in the Stanfields area. Parents were only concerned about your whereabouts when you were well overdue to return home. Our amusement was fairly mundane, but was played according to 'seasons' of the year.

'Jack Shine Your Lantern' involved getting a tin can and punching holes in it. You would then light a fire and fill the can full of hot coals, so that you had glowing embers in your tin can. Conkers was a great game. Every season, kids would come up with different recipes to make their conkers harder - whether they worked or not.

I remember playing football in Haywood Street with my elder cousin, when there were very few cars around. A policeman came by, and went absolutely ballistic with my cousin for playing football in an empty street. That's how severe they were in those days. Many of them were six foot four in height, and they could be very intimidating. They never harassed us, but we gave them a lot of respect and a wide berth. When we saw a helmet, we ran. It would be regarded as a scandal if a policeman knocked on your door - but people only reported you for serious acts of vandalism.

Another summer pastime was to make your own trolley, which incorporated four bicycle wheels and a seat. You could then sit in the trolley and whizz down Haywood Road, landing on the waste land at the bottom. You were probably travelling at about 30-40 mph.

Bycars Farm was still operating when I was a boy, and there was a lot of waste land adjacent. Much of this perhaps dated back over a century, and you would get spontaneous fires on it, caused by the shale. The whole area, of course, used to be riddled with mine shafts. I recall what I think was an old air shaft - a huge, circular tube lined with brick and of some depth. It was surrounded by rusty barbed wire, with coats hanging off it. We used to throw rubbish down it. They were highly dangerous and wouldn't be tolerated today, but I remember two behind our house.

There were also marlholes at Stanfields, and quite a deep one at Bycars which had an exposed seam of coal running through the side of it. This was probably about two feet thick. The poor people from the Stanfields council estate would regularly take a pram down to the marlhole and dig the coal out. However, there were dangers. One chap died when the side of the marlhole he was digging into collapsed on him. Another young boy drowned in a marlhole which had filled with water, just off Scotia Road[1].

At the age of about eleven, I encountered Vincent Riley, near to the new Vale Park ground. He was a very pleasant, toothless old chap, who offered my friends and I a drink of 'meths'. He was drunk out of his head, but we weren't frightened of him at all. I also remember the Burslem character Georgie King, a simple, very tall chap, who wore a trilby. During the Sixpenny Rush at the Burslem cinemas, he would be allowed to enter the area where the children sat at the front. The kids would chant, 'Georgie! Georgie! Georgie!' and he would react to this by having a tantrum.

Never mind today's vandalism - we were buggers as children. A favourite trick was to run through the Stanfields council house back gardens, which adjoined. We would smash our way through all the privet hedges. We did all sorts of stupid things with fireworks, making 'bazookas' by getting a copper tube, putting it in the ground and dropping an ignited banger down it as well as pebbles. Off it would go. Another trick, which harassed the neighbours, involved tying a banger to the stick of a rocket, two or three inches from the rocket burner. The rocket, when launched, would ignite the banger, and land somewhere locally. Friends and I would also use the Loop line train from Burslem to Tunstall, and throw stink-bombs out of the windows.

One of the great thrills of steam in those days was to stand on the railway bridge near Bycars and wait for the train to pass under. The steam would rush up on each side of the bridge, and the smell was indescribable. You would be enveloped in wonderful clouds of steam and smoke.

I was a pupil at Moorland Road School. There was sometimes spontaneous fighting on the playground, but if a fight was arranged between boys, you would go to a triangular piece of wasteland which we called the 'triangle'. This was located alongside the Loop line below Burslem Park. There are flats on site now.

I joined the scout group attached to the old Primitive Methodist chapel in High Lane. This has now been demolished. I remember being sent down by train to Deal on the South Coast with another scout. Our task was to set up a camp down there. I was only fourteen at the time.

When I was a little older, I joined in the 'monkey run', where you patrolled Queen Street, Market Place and Swan Bank, parading for girls. I only did this twice; I was told by one chap, 'If you come around here again, I'll smash your face in!' It was quite competitive. I also remember the youth who was often described as the first local teddy boy - Hugh Rennie, who came from the Newcastle area. Word would sometimes go around that he would be coming to the Queen's Hall for a dance. He had something of a reputation.

From the age of sixteen, I studied at the School of Art in Queen Street, regularly patronising the Queen's Head nearby with my friends. Arthur Berry used to sit in there, with his cap on. He was born in Smallthorne, but I think he aped the Potteries accent somewhat. He was an intelligent man who used to sit in the corner, pontificating.

However, my friends and I were only interested in drinking, girls and dancing at the time, and so Arthur, sporting his flat cap and muffler, was avoided. Two or three students began to copy his attire, wearing caps and mufflers - when you saw them together, they looked like the characters played by Peter Cooke and Dudley Moore.

As a student, my stamping ground was the jazz club in Waterloo Road. There was no alcohol sold on the premises, so you drank before you went in, exited midway through on your 'pass-out' and drank again, returned to the club, and drank again afterwards. It was a filthy place, and the walls ran with sweat - but it was a highlight for us on Fridays.

A big event in Burslem was the Arts Ball at the Queen's Hall. The students would take two months preparing huge sculptures for the hall, and we would go across and set it all out. Fancy dress was optional, and it was usually a fantastic night!

Notes:
(1) Compare this account with that of Alan Wood.

Moorland Road Junior School c.1953, prize daffodils. Jean Nevitt 2nd from left front row.
Sheila Bradley 3rd from right. Christine Wardle is wearing a collared white blouse.
Helen Smith is the dark-haired girl at the back. *Courtesy of Jean Wood.*

Park Road Secondary Modern School prefects 1959.
Jeant Nevitt, Head Girl, is in middle in cardigan. *Courtesy of Jean Wood (nee Nevitt).*

## 20. ALAN WOOD

Born William Alan Wood, 23/9/1940 in Tunstall. He grew up and was educated in Hamil Road, Burslem. When he was sixteen, the family moved to Coseley Street in Smallthorne. He married Jean Nevitt, a childhood friend, in 1966, and went to live in May Bank. An electrician by trade, he retired in 1997, having been employed at the Michelin tyre factory in Stoke.

Date of interview: 26/8/2003.

I was christened William Alan Wood, but I always preferred to be known as Alan. I was born in Tunstall but very soon afterwards moved with my mother to 169, Hamil Road, Burslem to live with my grandfather. My father, Wilfred Henry Wood, was in the Royal Air Force at the time. My mother was Evelyn May Wood (nee Stead). My earliest memories are of my mother going across to my grandmother Wood's house at Stanfield in Burslem. She washed clothes for grandmother once a week and Mother pushed me all the way there and back in my pram. I remember being pushed along one day, with the washing, and one of the wheels came off in Dolly's Lane. It stuck in my memory.

The Stanfield estate has been built there since, but there used to be quite a lot of open ground, as well as Finney's farm. Near to the allotments were two old mine workings in the vicinity of the Bycars farm. The two shafts were protected by wire, and we were not supposed to go near them, but we would throw stones down into them. We used to play around this area and pick coal which was to be found among the old colliery spoil which had been dumped. People also picked coal from out of a marlhole, which had a surviving rail track running down the side of it, presumably to assist in the excavating process. All this industrial activity provided us with a few nice slopes for tobogganing when it had snowed in the winter months.

There was a pool at Bycars, and we would fish there with a piece of cotton and a worm tied on the end. During one particularly warm summer, I recall that you could not put your feet down near the pool without frogs leaping out. On the top side of Dolly's Lane, towards where they later built the Stanfield Technical School, there was another pool where we fished for sticklebacks and newts. Old bricks used to be tipped, and there were also tin sheets from old Anderson shelters. Children would make huts from them.

We would also play in the cobbled back entries behind Hamil Road. We played cricket and football, and I learned to kick with my left foot because the ball would often roll into the gutter on the left hand side, and I would kick it out. So I learned to kick with my left foot as well as with my right.

In Hamil Road in the 1940s, there was Sambrook's builder's yard. This was located at the foot of the road on the left, if you were walking upbank. Further up, there were billboards which displayed posters, and then Kay's café. A fire station is there now. Still further on, was the British Road Service, a transport company, and just above it, a small PMT bus depot. All these establishments were in Hamil Road before Port Vale moved

Park Road Secondary Modern School 1956, probably 4th year. Eric Mountford, teacher, is far right. *Courtesy of Jean Wood.*

Park Road Secondary Modern School 1956, probably 2nd year. Teacher Graham Simons is pictured far left. *Courtesy of Jean Wood.*

there in 1950. Across the road and below Burslem Park, there was a triangle of waste ground upon which there are now blocks of flats. I remember bulldozers levelling the land in readiness for the construction of Vale Park. I had a friend who had a sandpit in his garden on account of his father being a builder. We would make terraces in the sand, just as the ones at Vale Park were being built.

I went to Jackfields Infant School in Burslem from the age of four or five. It being Wartime, there were air raid shelters in the school grounds, although I do not recall ever having to go into them. Just after the War had finished, there was a May Day celebration, and we children danced around a Maypole. My least favourite task at school involved having to stand up in front of the class and read aloud. I liked art. There was a paint store-room in the far corner of the school hall. From here, you would take your powder-paints, which you could mix with water. One year we decided to stage a school play in which I was asked to appear as a frog. I had a costume made out of two triangular sheets of cardboard or stiff green paper. There was room for my head and arms to stick out. However, I never appeared as the cardboard frog, as I was dropped from the play for clowning about too much.

In those days, pupils had a nap in the afternoon, and you would rest your head on your pump-bag. There was also concern about childrens' health, and we would be required to take cod liver oil and orange syrup. From the age of seven to eleven, I attended Moorland Road Junior School. At the back of the school on Lingard Street were wooden huts, incorporating about four classrooms. There was a veranda in front. The younger children took lessons in the huts, and pupils would often look out of the windows at the steam trains travelling along the adjacent railway line. Later, pupils left the huts and progressed to the main school, where teachers included Mr Forrester, Mr and Mrs Brammer, and Mr Liversage, a slight tyrant but a good teacher. The headmaster was Mr Light. I played football a couple of times for the school team, at left-back. Our goalkeeper was a bully at times, and on one occasion, he was yelling, *"Pass back! Pass back!"* I did, and he let the ball in. We used to play on the Sneyd cricket ground on Sneyd Hill.

Muffin the Mule was very popular when I was a child, and I walked into Burslem one Christmas in the hope of buying one of the puppets from the toy stall in the Covered Market. I didn't get one - our family couldn't afford it.

My last school was Park Road, and I stayed there until I was fifteen. In my first year, I finished second from top in my arithmetic class. I also managed to earn a geography prize. I recall Mr Simons, who taught music. One day, we pupils were listening to a radio programme on Bach, but Mr Simons realised that I was being inattentive. At the end of the lesson, he asked me, *"What was that programme about?"* Not having listened, I didn't know, so he gave the answer, *"Bach, lad, Bach!"* So I responded, *"Woof! Woof!"* I received the cane for that. Mr Shone took science, Mr Walker taught current affairs, and Mr Lake taught art. Miss Woollam was a form teacher who taught scripture, and she read to us from the Bible, which I thought was a wonderful story book.

Whilst still at school, I joined the Air Training Corps at the age of twelve or thirteen.

The squadron I joined was based at Cobridge, but there were several in the Potteries and Newcastle at the time. I was interested in aeroplanes, and I would sometimes cycle with a friend of mine to Meir aerodrome to watch the gliding on Sundays. I was also considering a career in the RAF. Ultimately, I just missed National Service, being slightly too young before it went. At the time, there was still National Service, so army cadets were trained for the army, sea cadets for the navy, and the ATC trained people for the Royal Air Force. We were trained to strip guns down and rebuild them, and studied map-reading and simple navigation. There would also be drills on Sunday mornings, and remembrance day parades, and there were excursions to summer camps at RAF stations. As a cadet, I rose to the position of sergeant.

Upon leaving school at Christmas, 1955, I joined G.H. Bates in Burslem as an apprentice electrician. Ironically, we still had gas-lighting in our house at Hamil Road. Bates had a small electrical shop off Waterloo Road, with an entry at the side leading to a yard to the rear. I joined electricians on jobs, learning the trade. However, there was sometimes less work in the winter months, and for this reason I only stayed for about two months. I was unemployed for six weeks before joining Hancock's electrical firm in Stoke.

At the age of about twenty, I ceased being an ATC cadet, but I eventually became a civilian instructor, helping with training and administration. My speciality was explaining about how helicopters worked. I was involved with the ATC part-time on two or three occasions per week until the 1970s.

Bank Hall Road, Burslem, looking towards Smallthorne, in 1964.
Emily Stanier and Florence Nevitt. *Courtesy of Jean Wood.*

The Coop store in Vivian Road, Burslem, c. 1935.

Doultons in Burslem, c.1935.

Potteries & District Directory 1912

A bit of Modern industrial Burslem. Looking up Bourne's Bank with Acme Marls on the left. (10/4/2001)

Crowds at the Burslem Festival in St John's Square. (3/5/1999)

Roy Evans and John Hegarty, playing in The Squeeze Box
folk band at the Leopard in Burslem. (27/7/2001)

Syd Lawton, licensee of the Swan in Burslem, being presented with a painting of the pub by Mervyn
Edwards. Harold Harper is far left; Ken Smith is far right. (25/2/2004)

## SOME CHURNET VALLEY TITLES STILL AVAILABLE

**BULLERS OF MILTON** Sue Taylor    plus 16 colour pages of Bullers' pottery £12.95

**JAMES HOLLAND** Steve Bond    Famous Victorian watercolourist from Burslem £ 9.95

**CALLING ALL CARS** Trevor Houlton  Memories of a M6 Motorway Policeman £ 7.95

**COUNTRYWISE ONE** Raymond Rush.  Illustrations by Gavin Clowes £ 6.95

**COUNTRYWISE TWO** Raymond Rush.  Illustrations by Gavin Clowes £ 6.95

**DISTINCTIVE SURNAMES OF N. STAFFS I:** Place names and landscape Edgar Tooth £ 9.95

**DISTINCTIVE SURNAMES OF N. STAFFS 2:** Occupations, trades, rank & office £9.95

**DURATION MAN** A.J. Heraty    A Staffordshire Soldier in the 1st World War £ 7.95

**ETRURIA: Jaspers, Joists and Jillivers**    Joan Morley £12.95

**FAMOUS WOMEN OF NORTH STAFFORDSHIRE** Patricia Pilling £ 6.95

**FARMERS AND POTTERS** An early Potteries' history    Gary Cooper £ 7.95

**WHEN I WAS A CHILD** Charles Shaw  A classic of Potteries' history (1904) £12.95

**RUDYARD REFLECTIONS** Basil Jeuda £ 7.95

**STAFFORDSHIRE REGIMENTS I 1705-1919** Dave Cooper £12.95

**STAFFORDSHIRE REGIMENTS II: 1705-1919** *"The Scrapbook"* Dave Cooper £12.95

**MILTON MEMORIES** Florence Chetwin and Margaret Reynolds £ 8.95

**MONASTIC STAFFORDSHIRE** John Tomkinson Religious houses of the County £12.95

**MOTHER BURSLEM** Bertram Hodgkiss  An in depth history to 1910 £14.95

**SILVERDALE: LIFE ON THE DALE** Barry Williams £ 8.95

**STAFFORDSHIRE LEGENDS** Alan Gibson £ 8.95

**ST EDWARD'S HOSPITAL, CHEDDLETON** Max Chadwick and Dave Pearson £20.00

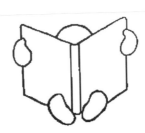